Evangelical Christian Women

QUALITATIVE STUDIES IN RELIGION

GENERAL EDITORS: Penny Edgell Becker *and* Mary Jo Neitz

The Qualitative Studies in Religion series was founded to make a place for careful, sustained, engaged reflection on the link between the kinds of qualitative methods being used and the resulting shape, tone, and substance of our empirical work on religion. We seek to showcase a wide range of qualitative methodologies, including ethnography; analysis of religious texts, discourses, rituals, and daily practices; in-depth interviews and life histories; and narrative analyses. We present empirical studies from diverse disciplines that address a particular problem or argument in the study of religion. We welcome a variety of approaches, including those drawing on multiple qualitative methods or combining qualitative and quantitative methods. We believe that excellent empirical studies can best further a critical discussion of the links among methods, epistemology, and social scientific theory and thereby help to reconceptualize core problems and to advance our understanding of religion and society.

Evangelical Christian Women: War Stories in the Gender Battles
Julie Ingersoll

Evangelical Christian Women

War Stories in the Gender Battles

Julie Ingersoll

NEW YORK UNIVERSITY PRESS

New York and London

NEW YORK UNIVERSITY PRESS
New York and London
www.nyupress.org

Library of Congress Cataloging-in-Publication Data
Ingersoll, Julie.
Evangelical Christian women :
war stories in the gender battles / Julie Ingersoll
p. cm. — (Qualitative studies in religion)
Includes bibliographical references and index.
ISBN 0–8147–3769–2 (alk. paper) —
ISBN 0–8147–3770–6 (pbk : alk. paper)
1. Women in fundamentalist churches—History—20th century.
2. Sex role—Religious Aspects—Christianity—History of doctrines—20th century.
3. Protestant women—United States—History—20th century.
4. Evangelicalism—United States—History—20th century. I. Title. II. Series.
BX7800.F864I54 2003
280'.4'0820973—dc22 2003016366

New York University Press books are printed on acid-free paper,
and their binding materials are chosen for strength and durability.

Manufactured in the United States of America

10 9 8 7 6 5 4 3 2 1

For my parents,
who encouraged my incessant questions.

Contents

Acknowledgments

Writing the acknowledgments section of this book is at once gratifying and daunting. It is an opportunity to reflect on many years of friendship and collegiality; at the same time, it is a task I know I can never adequately perform.

My first offer of thanks has to go to the many people who opened their lives (and sometimes their homes) to tell me their stories; some of them are named within, and others are not. Without them, there would be no book. I hope that I have presented the many things they shared with me in ways that honor them and their lives.

Second only to the people whose stories I've told, I want to thank Wade Clark Roof and Terry Roof. Clark was my mentor at the University of California, where he supervised this research as my doctoral dissertation. He and Terry built a community among UCSB graduate students that shaped me as a scholar and as a person.

Several people have read this manuscript and offered valuable feedback for which I am grateful. Of course, the first of these were my additional dissertation committee members: Phillip Hammond, the late Walter Capps, and Catherine Albanese. Friends and colleagues who have read part or all of the manuscript include Diana Garland, Diana Butler-Bass, Russell T. McCutcheon, Edward Linenthal, Betty DeBerg, and the editors of this series, Mary Jo Neitz and Penny Egdell. Their encouragement and gentle criticism have made this book tremendously better. Parts of this analysis also appeared in a volume entitled *Personal Knowledge and Beyond*, edited by J. Shawn Landres, James Spickard, and Meredith McQuire, each of whom helped me clarify my arguments and improved the analysis of this larger project.

I have benefited greatly from an ongoing conversation with friends and colleagues: first, those with the UCSB Religious Studies Program, in particular the faculty, several alumni, and my own contemporaries; second, those at the Society for the Scientific Study of Religion, where I have, since my second year of graduate school, presented my work; third, the members of the Faculty Seminar at the University of North Florida. Thanks to you all for challenging me to think in new ways by commenting on my work, by exposing me to yours, and, most important, by offering your friendship.

Members and leaders of several organizations assisted in my research, including Christians for Biblical Equality, the Hestenes Center for Christian Women in Leadership, the Evangelical Women's Caucus, and the Oregon Extension of Houghton College. They opened their libraries, helped me make important contacts, and often also provided hospitality as I traveled to do research.

My dissertation research was generously supported by grants from the following institutions: the University of California Santa Barbara Affiliates; the Society for the Scientific Study of Religion; Re-Forming the Center Project, at Messiah College, which was, in turn, funded by the Lilly Endowment; the Religion in Los Angeles Project, funded by the Pew Charitable Trusts; the Louisville Institute; and Southwest Missouri State University.

Jennifer Hammer, my editor at New York University Press, deserves much credit for seeing this project to completion. Several years ago, Jennifer contacted me after learning of a paper I was presenting at a conference. She was building a Religious Studies list and had taken a long view of things, to say the least. She stayed in touch with me through the years of research, writing, graduation, and then distractions as I took a series of temporary teaching positions. She gently kept me on track without adding to the guilt I already felt about not doing things as quickly as I thought I should.

The material in this book has made its way into classrooms at Millsaps College, Rhodes College, Southwest Missouri State University, and the University of North Florida. Students are always quick to question conventional scholarly wisdom, and they keep me (and my work) real.

Finally, Arminius (the dog, not the theologian) who has been my companion for nearly fifteen years.

My deepest thanks to you all.

Introduction

But as I started thinking through all this . . . I got seriously suicidal on several occasions. This spring, I just thought about taking huge doses of antidepressants. There were several times I had just made up my mind that this was "it." Then it dawned on me. I began to understand where my theology was leading me: God created me a woman. That was His choice. Somebody, somewhere along the line at creation gave me those gifts—I really am a preacher and a teacher. And the one place in my life I wanted to exercise what I am is in the Church, because that was the thing I loved the best. But although God created me a woman and, one must assume, gave me those [teaching and preaching] gifts, He also makes it impossible for me to please Him. Because to please Him would be to exercise the fullness of who I am, I can't please Him in the institution that represents Him. So the only way, ultimately, that I could please God would be to kill myself. Because nothing I could ever do as a living human being, because of being a woman, could ever please God.

—Sandra, a faculty member at a conservative seminary

Tears welled in my own eyes as Sandra described her journey from her early years as a woman so committed to her faith that she chose to devote her life to it to a despair so complete that she wasn't sure she wanted to continue to live at all. Sandra's story was one of the more poignant I encountered in my research among conservative Protestant women, but it was not unique.

This book examines gender as a core aspect of culture in American Protestant fundamentalism. It seeks to go beyond current work on this topic by moving from an effort to find women's empowerment amid structural limitations to exploring the experiences of women in the subculture who participate in the process of change. This is not a feminist critique from outside the tradition; neither is it a search for hidden forms of empowerment. It is a sociological study of conservative women who challenge gender norms within their religious traditions, of the fallout they experience as part of the ensuing conflict, and of the significance of the conflict over gender for the development and character of culture.

I met Sandra, as I met many of the women I interviewed, at a conference sponsored by the Center for Christian Women in Leadership at Eastern College, a conference held for the express purpose of giving women like Sandra tools to avoid gender-related conflict and support when such conflict found them nonetheless. The work of the center was deemed necessary because, by the late 1990s (despite harsh rhetoric to the contrary), conservative Christian women were serving in ministry positions in conservative institutions across the country.

Antifeminism may be the dominant perspective in this conservative Christian subculture, but it has long been challenged by alternative voices that argue for women's equality. Throughout the 1970s, as the women's movement was gaining ground in the larger culture, evangelical feminism (also known as Christian feminism or biblical feminism) grew in significance and became a powerful force in this conservative Christian world. Two generations of evangelical Christian women have now grown up believing that God could and did call women to ministry; that God had plans for their lives and that he had gifted them accordingly; that they were obligated to God to use wisely the gifts and talents He had given them; that marriage was intended to be a partnership of equals; and that parenting was the most serious calling given to both women and men.

Those women flocked to Christian colleges and then to graduate schools and seminaries. They became teachers, pastors, professors, and scholars. They believed, perhaps naively, that their sense of calling, their hard work, and their devotion to their faith would be respected and valued in their Christian subculture. And, from many, they did receive encouragement and support.

But conservative Christianity is a subculture divided over the very issue of women's proper roles, and when these women moved into positions of respect, authority, and responsibility they encountered difficulties they could not have anticipated and for which they were not prepared.

In "What It Means to Go First: Clergywomen of the Pioneer Generation," Joy Charlton explores "incidences where [women pastors] were told directly and indirectly that being a woman in the professional role was unusual, incidences where they still hear the theological argument against women's ordination, jokes made at their expense, [and] situations they define as sexual harassment." These women were referring not to occasional slights and innocent comments but rather to a constant and pervasive pattern of behavior that undermined their ability to do their ministry jobs. Charlton observed the extent to which scholars often note the war stories but then gloss over them to move on to other issues.[1] My study addresses that gap in scholarship by documenting and exploring these war stories. In the face of a growing number of scholarly studies of conservative religious women that argue that submission is somehow "really" empowerment, this book seeks to get at the other side of the story—to document and explore the experiences of the women caught in the middle of the conservative Christian culture war over gender.

Recent scholarship on women in American conservative religion has shown how some women recast the conservative doctrine of women's submission in ways that are ultimately empowering. Often with a focus on converts, these studies have asked, "How is it that women would choose to embrace a religious tradition that is predicated on their own loss of power and seeming oppression?" Scholars have begun with the assumption that the experiences conservative women claim for themselves are authentic and that (despite how we might feel were we part of such traditions) the women who choose these life courses do so because they find something of value in them; specifically, they argue that what looks like powerlessness from the outside has its own processes of empowerment.

For example, in *God's Daughters: Evangelical Women and the Power of Submission*,[2] R. Marie Griffith argues that if we look at the practical outworkings of the doctrine of submission in the lives of pentecostal women, instead of just the doctrine as it is articulated by religious leaders, we can see ways in which those women reshape submission to create a space of empowerment. Griffith's approach goes a long way in helping us to take seriously the convictions and values of these conservative women without dismissing their viewpoint as some form of "false consciousness" and, for this reason, is an important contribution to this growing list of titles on women in conservative religion.

Griffith began her fieldwork in the pentecostal women's prayer and devotional organization Women's Aglow Fellowship with an interest in the prayer lives of women. Over time, however, her study came to explore a multitude of other issues as well, including gender and power relationships, the role of religion in a therapeutic culture and the impact of the therapeutic culture on religion, the history and ethos of Women's Aglow, and the themes of healing, transformation, secrecy, and intimacy as they play themselves out in the experience of the women in Women's Aglow. She paints a textured picture of the lives of the women in Women's Aglow, and most of the time that picture fits with what we might expect from women in an international pentecostal prayer organization. But Griffith gives a surprising twist to her narrative as she pieces together her argument that, to these women, submission is really freedom, that, in actuality, it is empowerment.

She grants that the doctrines of submission have softened over time as religious leaders have emphasized the loving character of "responsible male headship." But Griffith doesn't hide the fact that significant differences exist between the forms of "empowerment" available to Aglow women and feminist notions of equality. As Aglow women confess their dissatisfaction with their lives, they still do so in ways that conform to accepted narrative conventions that assume that "domestic unhappiness stems largely from stubborn willfulness, so that healing can occur only when a wife pliantly consents to obey her husband and let him reign as leader of the home."[3]

So how is it that submission is inverted, transformed into empowerment? When exploring the related issue of weight control, Griffith explains: "surrender and discipline appear to harmonize as the will of God is internalized in the will of the individual. . . . "[4] And she does not miss the point that, in this subculture, the power in submission applies to all Christians, not just to women, as she calls our attention to the "paradox of surrender and control so deeply ingrained in evangelicalism."[5]

But there are hints throughout that, although hidden from view by the Aglow rhetoric, there are other forces at play, as well. Griffith points to the significant "lampooning of male behavior" and the jokes about "men's 'nature' that have a rather sharp edge."[6] In her insightful discussion of the impact of the "therapeutic culture" on the women she studies, Griffith explores evasion and denial of anger (her example is a case in which a woman forgave a man who had raped her). Griffith recognized that the stories the women tell "end on a more cheerful note than their subject(s) might warrant."[7] Indeed, she writes, "all narratives end with joyful professions of victory and transformation."[8] Those to whom she gives voice (and those to whom the organization gives voice) tell their stories in the institutionally approved narrative format. Whatever the problem, the love of Jesus has overcome it. But a reader is left wondering whether the biting humor might not be an outlet for otherwise "inappropriate" expression of anger.

Despite the seeming autonomy of Aglow, a women's ministry, it is over-seen by a board of advisers that is all male. Griffith documents the variety of explanations for this fact, as well as the variety of views on the role the board actually plays.[9] But, with some women leaders believing that the board's role is merely symbolic while others believe that the men oversee Aglow's theology as a "protection and covering," it seems inevitable that there would be conflicts over control. Griffith's narrative left me wondering how this really works and whether all the women are equally happy with it.

Griffith deals adeptly with two groups of people: women in conservative Protestantism who embrace patriarchy and submission, and feminists outside those traditions who insist on understanding the conservative women on their own (feminist) terms. But she gives no voice to the women within the tradition who have chafed under patriarchy—those who have been sometimes nearly destroyed by it. Evangelical feminists (and those who have studied them)[10] have documented the larger number of conservative Protestant women (including evangelicals, pentecostals, charismatics, and fundamentalists) who find it difficult to reconcile what they are taught about the Bible with what they believe to be true about their own identities and callings.

In *Godly Women: Fundamentalism and Female Power*,[11] Brenda Brasher gives depth and nuance to the literature on the lives of conservative Christian women. She struggles to step out of her own world and into theirs, presenting their stories much as they might tell them. She finds that, while the women she studies are excluded from congregational authority, they are by no means without power. Brasher effectively demonstrates the significant differences between authority and power, shows the workings of female power in the congregations she studies, and then explains that this is in large measure a result of the highly developed network created by the women's ministry enclaves. In her words, "the . . . primary thesis of this book is that to Christian Fundamentalist women, the restrictive religious identity they embrace improves their ability to direct the course of their lives and empowers them in their relationships with others."[12] And, she writes, "again, women's interviews divulge how submission increases rather than decreases a woman's power in the marital relationship."[13]

But here, too, there are hints that the story is more complicated. For example, by Brasher's own account, the separate women's sphere in which these conservative Christian women find empowerment includes only a fraction of church women—one-third of the women in one congregation

and one-fifth of the women in the other.[14] Brasher hints at "communal social pressures" faced by these women but doesn't elaborate on what those
might be. She refers to "rebellious impulses" but doesn't spell them out.[15]
She says that she believes the women spoke openly[16] but never explains
why she believes this to be true. Given the emphasis conservative Christians place on making a positive witness of their faith, there are significant
forces that obfuscate tension, conflict, and disagreement. Brasher even
notes that her respondents told her repeatedly that they valued the opportunity to have their "testimonies" "on the record."[17] If the stories of these
women had been told from a different perspective, emphasizing the variety of voices to be found within this world, Brasher would have asked how
much this motivation to have "testimonies" on the record had led the
women to sanitize their views on gender issues so as to not draw attention
away from their emphasis on the necessity of a "personal relationship with
Jesus." When Brasher describes how, at one point during her research, a female women's pastor deferred to a decision made by the male pastor and
everyone said that the woman's decision was an autonomous one, Brasher
suggests that this seemed implausible and that an accurate reading of the
politics of the situation "eluded" her.[18] In another incident, when women
in one congregation drew on their enclave power to influence a pastoral
decision, Brasher even notes that she doesn't believe she would have
learned the details of the story had she not actually been there.[19]

So when women claim that the restrictions put on them "do not bother
[them] because [they] don't find [them] limiting," or that being banned
from pastoral ministry or church governing positions doesn't keep them
from "meaningful religious participation,"[20] a discerning reader is left to
wonder whether the respondents are being completely straightforward. In
other words, the women have reasons to tell their stories in ways that
deemphasize gender conflict, and it is likely that there are issues not visible
to an "outsider" researcher.

And then there are specific instances that beg for more elaboration.
When one church went back and forth on the question of whether women
could lead the house churches,[21] there was no real discussion of how the
ousted women really felt; when the pastor at the other church limited
working hours for staff women with children, the decision was clearly un-
popular.[22] Did all of the women just fall into line on these points, or were
there conflicts to which an outsider could never be privy?

In one example where the women did not "fall into line," Brasher explores the fallout from a situation in which a pastor became inappropri-

ately involved with a woman he was counseling. The pastors' wives then led an effort to eliminate the practice of having male pastors counsel female parishioners. This was represented as an example of the successful exercise of female power. The pastors' wives first began to teach the other women in the church that women shouldn't seek counsel from men because the men didn't understand their problems anyway. "Don't cast your jewels before them," one of the women taught in Bible study. Brasher did not comment on or elaborate on the hostility implicit in the statement. The women's pastor was referring to the biblical passage, "Don't cast your pearls before swine." She was, in effect, calling the male pastors pigs. Furthermore, while the pastors' wives prevailed in this conflict, it is a bit more ambiguous whether the women generally benefited. Women who do not necessarily feel "better understood" by other women lost their choice as to whom to seek for counseling; women could no longer seek the counsel of those with the most training and experience; and, as a result of this decision, women had even less access to those in the congregation who held most of the authority.

Brasher mentions a few women who expressed some dissatisfaction with the gender norms and expectations (e.g., they complained about sermons that "harped" on submission and expressed support for alternative styles of family and equality within marriage) but did not follow up on these stories. I am now advocating a subsequent move: having taken seriously what Brasher's women say about their lives, we now need to take seriously the alternative voices.

When I have used these works in the classroom, many of my students, having grown up in fundamentalist traditions, object that the arguments in them just don't ring true. They know from experience that many women in these traditions do not find "power in submission," that women often feel limited, discounted, and redirected, when they express the sense of calling for which men are encouraged and rewarded. Many know all too well that women in these traditions struggle with frustration and depression as a result of their gendered worlds.

My students are correct, and my own research suggests that, while the authors' findings are certainly true for some (even many) women in these communities, the story is much more complicated than current studies indicate and that many women do not find such empowerment. While they contribute to our developing understanding of conservative religious women in important respects, current studies miss the stories of many other women in these traditions. This not only marginalizes alternative views but also masks important aspects of religious phenomena.[23] In this case, the preference for an integrated view of women's religion (presented primarily by the women in power, who have a vested interest in the legitimization of the existing structures and practices) over the messier, complex reality lived by women in contested positions creates a distorted view of women in conservative Protestantism.

In reality, gender norms, expectations, and ideology are always in social process, and that process is a creative, dialectical one in which no one group is completely in control. In fact, the group boundaries themselves are always changing. Sites of conflict over gender ideology serve as windows into the process of cultural production of a symbol that is both religious and cultural. Current feminist scholarship, which emphasizes "giving voice to the Other," has had the paradoxical effect of silencing the feminist women within these traditions.

It is my argument that until ethnographers (specifically those who study women in conservative religious traditions) incorporate the conflict and complexity that characterizes gender norms, expectations, and ideology in these traditions, we will miss an opportunity to observe the process by which the cultures produce and reproduce themselves. Factions with the most power inevitably try to create the illusion that theirs is the only possible interpretation of reality. By failing to tease out the hidden counterhegemonic voices, we become complicit in their effort to maintain the status quo.[24]

Methods and Sources

This study is based on an extensive collection of primary-source materials and considerable field research. I have drawn on books, magazine articles, newsletters, and journals, as well as the personal correspondence files of several of my respondents.[25] I was also given access to the entire institutional archives of Christians for Biblical Equality. I spent more than two years between 1993 and 1995 conducting the formal field research, which included forty-four in-depth formal interviews in several different cities and an uncountable number of informal interviews and conversations. Over a longer period I spent time as a participant observer at churches, conferences, seminars, and activities at other Christian colleges and seminaries.

As I gathered stories from evangelical women, I was amazed by the prevalence of the conflicts over gender. Whenever I asked evangelical women whether they knew of such stories, they indicated that they knew of several. In the course of my field research, I encountered innumerable people who said, "Do I have a story for you!" Many others said, "you really should talk to . . ." and then gave me a name and phone number. Some of those stories are recorded here, while many are not. The women who had endured the conflicts were extremely generous, not only with their time but also in their willingness to revisit clearly painful experiences. Despite evangelical concerns about presenting a positive picture of the community to outsiders, no one ever said, "I've never heard of such things" (though I'm sure there are some who would). On the contrary, I have collected many more stories than I could possibly use and have chosen not to follow up on leads to still others out of the necessity of bringing this project to completion. In reality, the themes in each story became so familiar that I felt that to include more examples of the same issues would be redundant. I have also avoided assessing the specific situations to try to identify "what really happened." Rather, my interest is in the women's perceptions about the conflicts they faced and the significance of those perceived conflicts for the subculture and our understanding of it. I learned early on that the stories themselves were still so hotly contested that, in any case, such assessment would be impossible. I anticipate that some will be offended by this book. I also anticipate that many others, those who have been told they were imagining things or were being "overly sensitive" in the midst of conflict, will be pleased and gratified that these stories have been told.

It seems appropriate, at this point, to make clear the extent of my personal involvement in these stories. Some of the women about whom I write came to me because they had heard about my research and wanted to tell their stories. A couple of the women are women I know very well, and several of them are women I knew of and admired long before I had the chance to talk with them in the course of my research.

In a very real sense, though, none of these stories is mine. Although I studied briefly at a seminary, I have had no significant connection with any evangelical schools, and I never considered entering the pastoral ministry. Aside from a sojourn through the conservative Christian world, I maintain no ties to that community. I watched as a close friend lived through a situation like those I describe (coincidentally after my research for this project was well under way), but for reasons both academic and legal I have not drawn significantly on her experience in my examples. I have no further personal role in the conflicts included in this study.

On the other hand, my interest in this topic does come directly from my own life experiences. From the early 1980s through the early 1990s, I was an active part of the conservative Christian world about which I now write; I belonged to several churches in different parts of the country that I would now label fundamentalist, and I was a student at Fuller Theological Seminary in Pasadena, California. Fuller was, by this time, clearly a part of the larger evangelical world, though there were still fundamentalist factions to be found there. I was in a nonministry track, although there were many women happily studying to be ministers. During my years as a part of that world, my commitment to feminism remained constant. That commitment, as well as my own goals and ambitions, was a persistent source of conflict and tension. I bristled at interpretations of the Bible that seemed to me to say that God saw women as inferior to men. Yet those interpretations were so pervasive (and oft repeated) that there seemed to me to be no other possibility—until, one day, my new fundamentalist (male) pastor said to me, "What do you think the Bible really says about women?" I'm sure at that point I rolled my eyes. I remember steeling myself for the anticipated onslaught. Instead, he handed me the first "biblical feminist" book I had ever seen: *Women at the Crossroads,* by Kari Torjesen Malcolm. Malcolm had been raised as a missionary kid (the authority and autonomy given to women on the mission field, as compared to the limitations placed on women at home, has been widely noted), and when she came to the United States she discovered that churches here had very different expectations of her. The book traces her despair at trying to adjust and her own discovery of an alternative view within her biblically oriented tradition. It culminates with her discussion of her new sense of calling and her efforts to share this view with other women. The sense of relief I felt at reading her story is indescribable. I soon acquired an extensive library on the topic. In hindsight, I see this as the beginning of my break with that tradition. I relay this story here because I heard similar stories over and over again from the women I interviewed. Whether they encountered biblical feminism in a book, in an organization like Christians for Biblical Equality, or (more rarely) from a sermon, they all describe their sense of freedom and relief in similar terms.

When the women I interviewed told me of the despair they had experienced over the fact that they could not reconcile who they were with what they saw as the demands of God, I knew firsthand what they meant. And it was undoubtedly a desire to make some sense of my own background that drew me to this project. I recognize that my position as a former insider means that I inevitably bring my own experience to bear on my research. On the other hand, the experiences out of which these stories flow are pervasive in the conservative Protestant subculture, and I wonder whether a researcher with no insider experience could come to see the problems as these women do.

Despite having been an insider during early adulthood, I am now an outsider. Not only am I now a trained academic; I also no longer share these folks' religious worldview, political commitments, and community ties as I once did. I understand the stories of the women I have studied through a lens shaped by my training, my status as a former insider, and my status as a current outsider. I can illustrate the way in which this reality shapes my analysis with a brief story about the development of this book over time. I began this formal research as a graduate student. As I presented aspects of this project in various academic forums, my colleagues repeatedly asked one question: Why don't these women just leave? I attempted to answer, but the question always seemed strange to me. The option of "just leaving" doesn't make sense in this world, and it didn't occur to me that it was an option for my subjects. As the study progressed, I moved further and further from that conservative Christian world until ultimately my study was my only remaining tie to it. As this happened, the idea of leaving made more and more sense to me. I had moved from thinking (in agreement with those I was studying) that leaving was not really an option to seeing the changed lives of some who did leave, and being able to reflect on why some leave and some stay, as well as the cultural resources that allow those who leave to do so.

While conducting this research several years ago, I was closer to the evangelical world than I am now. I intuitively reacted to some situations like the women in my study. I have noted some of these experiences in the pages that follow. As I write this now, though, I feel completely distanced from this world.

Terminology

The study of American evangelicalism is fraught with difficulties over definitions and terminology.[26] Definitions for "evangelical" are elusive, and the usage of the terms "liberal" and "conservative" are so contextual (and even politicized) that they grow increasingly problematic. Alternative terms are no better. With each attempt at definition, there are the inevitable groups that "seem to be" evangelical but are ruled out, because of some view they hold or some practice they embrace. If evangelicals and fundamentalists are conservative Protestants, then what do we do with the "evangelical left"? If they are premillennialists, what do we do with postmillennial Christian Reconstructionists and other conservative Christians who embrace postmillennialism and dominion theology? If we uncritically accept fundamentalists' self-definition as "literalist," we unwittingly lend support to some conservative Christians in their conflicts with other conservative Christians.[27] Additionally, the line between those who seem best labeled "fundamentalist" and those who might be better labeled "evangelical" is blurred and even seems to move depending on the issue under consideration.[28]

The convention among observers of conservative American Protestantism has been to reserve the term "fundamentalist" for the most conservative in that community, while those who identify with the broader movement are termed "evangelicals." The current usage of the terms "fundamentalist" and "evangelical" dates from the 1920s and 1940s, respectively. Fundamentalism's rise at the beginning of the twentieth century was largely a response to the developments of modernism and growing pluralism. It took its name from the series of pamphlets "The Fundamentals."[29] The fundamentalism of the 1920s was characterized by an emphasis on traditional Christian teachings (the Deity of Christ, the literal truth of the miracles recorded in the Bible, the virgin birth, and so forth), premillennial dispensationalism, revivalism, traditional gender norms, and separation from the world. Evangelicalism, in its current incarnation, developed in the 1940s as an effort to reform fundamentalism. Sometimes called "neo-evangelicals," the 1940s evangelicals held much the same doctrinal views as the fundamentalists, but their understanding of the relationship between the church and the larger culture was different. Rejecting fundamentalist "separationism," evangelicals in the 1940s sought to engage culture and transform it—to *evangelize* it.[30]

Unfortunately, as we moved into the second half of the twentieth century, observers of these movements sought to retain the same terms, struggling to support definitions of the groups as though they were frozen in time. Key observers of the late-twentieth-century development of the conservative Christian subculture emphasized intellectual history over cultural history. Thus, the most influential definitions focused on theological differences and distinctions. Even worse, in some cases, other observers used the term "fundamentalist" derisively to refer to any relatively conservative tradition (that is, "conservative" relative to the speaker's own perspective). Often, strained attempts at definition resulted in a defeated retreat to "Well, you know one when you see one." Barbara Wheeler then challenged us to take "you know one when you see one" seriously and to look at just *what we see* when we know we are looking at an evangelical.[31]

Wheeler suggests that observers of evangelicalism consider that "it is not doctrine or ancestry or warm family feeling . . . but religious culture." Maybe, she continues, "the best definition of an evangelical is someone who understands its argot, knows where to buy posters with Bible verses on them, and recognizes names like James Dobson and Frank Peretti." Wheeler points to the distinctively evangelical religious dialect, leaders and celebrities, self-help groups, and Christian service providers (e.g., chiropractors and dentists), as well as the extensive material culture of music, tee-shirts, bumper stickers, books, and jewelry, as evidence that evangelicals are culture makers.

Susan Harding pursued this cultural definition in her groundbreaking work on the rhetoric of Jerry Falwell, showing how fundamentalists and evangelicals united to form a movement that was similar to, and at the same time different from, both movements as they had existed in the first half of the century.[32] Harding shows how fundamentalists in Falwell's camp remade themselves:

> The people I saw and talked to [at Falwell's church] struck me not as tradition-bound, defensive, or fearful, but as people aggressively asserting and reshaping themselves and their world against any and all who resisted them. Far from bunkering themselves, these fundamentalists seemed to have a vast appetite for worldly ideas and practices—sports, therapy, sex manual, politics, glossy magazines, television.[33]

Both Wheeler and Harding call us to understand this movement as a cultural one rather than as one that can be understood primarily in terms of doctrine and theology. Contemporary conservative Christians may have much in common with their theological and cultural ancestors in America, but they are also a distinctive subculture that could have developed only at the end of the twentieth century.

This book is about the people who recognize the names Dobson and Peretti as the people at Falwell's church do; it is about the conservative

Christian subculture that came together in the late 1970s and 1980s in North America in an effort to reshape the world according to their understanding of the Bible. I call this alternatively "the conservative Christian subculture" and "the conservative Protestant movement," recognizing the complications and limitations of doing so. When citing various sources (both primary and secondary), I use the term as it is in the original. "Liberal" and "conservative" are used as they are commonly understood in contemporary American politics to denote perspectives on political and social issues, with the recognition that few people fit neatly within either camp. And, perhaps more important, the terms themselves make sense only in specific contexts.[34]

Likewise, the relationship between the terms "evangelicalism" and "feminism" is fraught with difficulty. In what follows, the terms "Christian feminist," "biblical feminist," and "evangelical feminist" are used interchangeably. While there are those who would take issue with this usage (most notably other feminists who wonder how any version of conservative Christianity can be considered feminist), and others have chosen to use only one of these terms to describe themselves for one reason or another, those feminists with whom I am centrally concerned and their primary opponents within the subculture use all three terms.[35]

Despite current popular perspectives, women have long served as religious leaders in evangelical and even fundamentalist churches. Today's conservative Protestant movement itself represents a blending of at least two Protestant traditions that tend toward different views on women's leadership—the pietistic traditions that emphasize religious experience and personal piety and have encouraged women in leadership, and the reformed traditions, which emphasize theology and doctrine and have discouraged women's leadership.[36] The evangelical commitment to "engage the larger culture"[37] leads many evangelicals to be sympathetic to the pleas of women for greater equality; changing cultural attitudes toward women's roles and limitations have also influenced the conservative Protestant movement. The result is complex, conflicted, and often paradoxical attitudes and behaviors within the movement regarding women religious leaders. And, because changes in cultural norms (including changes in gender norms) happen in fits and starts over long periods of time, a number of women are caught in the middle of the transformation; if we accept the "culture wars" metaphor, these women are caught in the crossfire. Despite the limitations of a "culture wars" theory for modeling all of American Protestantism, let alone all of American culture, the prevalence of the notion that we are in the midst of a war persists. This is in part a result of the readiness with which we can find examples of vocal soldiers who represent polarized factions in almost every public debate. While the conceptualization of the cultural conflict as warlike may be disturbing, the analogy of a front line seems appropriate to describe the experiences of the women I studied. They do talk about "war stories," they feel embattled, and they carry with them scars that include experiences of broken families, derailed careers, and, sometimes, abandoned spiritual lives. They suffer from fatigue, despair, cynicism, and emotional distress that often reach the level of clinical depression. They sometimes even long for death. More subtle "culture wars" analyses have argued that divisions are found more often within traditions than between traditions that represent different factions in the larger culture.[38]

Gender issues remain profoundly divisive as America enters the twenty-first century. In many quarters (among both conservatives and liberals), an individual's views regarding women's roles are used as a litmus test to determine whether the person is "one of us" or "one of them." Scholarly portrayals of gender issues in American evangelicalism and fundamentalism sometimes contribute to this polarization.

Conservative Protestantism is often portrayed by scholars as uniformly committed to "traditional family values" and to the antifeminism therein. Differing views on gender within the subculture are commonly explained away as aberrations or accommodations to greater cultural forces,[39] rather than being seen as legitimate alternatives that are part of a process of definition and deserving of recognition. This monolithic Protestant traditionalism is then portrayed as a central force on one side of a larger culture war: conservatives (including evangelicals and fundamentalists) versus liberals (including feminists).[40] This polarized view plays into the hands both of those who want to demonize conservative Protestantism and of conservative Protestant "traditionalists" who want to claim that theirs is the only legitimate position within a "biblical" (by which they mean a conservative Protestant interpretation of the Bible) worldview.

A more nuanced picture of evangelical gender ideology has begun to emerge, and scholars are increasingly recognizing that gender is (and has been) a contested category, even within this conservative subculture that has attempted to present a "united front" to the world on issues relating to gender.[41] However, despite the recognition among scholars that patriarchalism has long been disputed, little work has examined the conflict that has ensued within the subculture itself as "feminists" and "traditionalists" battle to return conservative Protestantism to their respective mythic views of the past.[42] This study begins with the assumption that evangelicalism is, among other things, a cultural system, a set of symbols that act as a rubric for ordering life and providing meaning. I argue that the way in which meaning is symbolized is neither purely individual nor purely communal; it arises out of a dialectical process between individuals and their religious subculture. My thesis is threefold. First, gender is a central organizing principle and a core symbolic system in this subculture. Second, the interpretation and control of that symbol is not fixed and permanent but, on the contrary, is the result of an ongoing process of construction (production), which entails a tremendous degree of negotiation. Third, at least in the case of gender issues in the evangelical subculture, the dialectical process of symbolizing meaning is essentially characterized by conflict.

The ways in which conservative Christian men and women understand their gender identities, the ways in which they believe they ought to relate to each other, and the ways in which they do, in fact, relate to each other are tremendously complicated. While ideological constructions often seem clear-cut and simple, the demands of the modern world require a level of fluidity. We begin by exploring the various dimensions of conservative Christian gender culture. By "gender culture" I mean the combination of theology, ideology, practices, norms, expectations, and all other dimensions of gender as they exist in conservative Protestantism.

Competing Theologies

Those Christians in the traditional camp on issues of gender cover a broad spectrum.[43] At one end are those who view male headship in marriage as primarily symbolic and who permit women to participate in church leadership but bar them from the position of head pastor. At the other end of the spectrum are those who draw clear and absolute demarcations between men and women in almost every dimension of life. There is also diversity of opinion within evangelical feminism. Some of the more liberal evangelical feminists identify with the "evangelical left" and support a broad agenda with which many secular feminists would identify. At the other end of the spectrum are evangelical feminists who focus their efforts almost exclusively on gaining functional equality of opportunity. These feminists often agree with everything traditionalists believe, with the exception of the points relating to gender roles.

It is the more conservative of the two perspectives, the relatively extreme traditionalists and relatively moderate feminists, who have directly engaged each other in debate and who are most thoroughly dealt with here.[44]

Traditionalist evangelicals and fundamentalists pride themselves on laying out a clear, concrete, unchanging blueprint for gender distinctions. They believe that wives should submit to their husbands, who should lovingly lead their families; that pastoral authority and church leadership roles are prohibited to women; and that, when possible, women should find their callings at home caring for their families. They ground this perspective in the variety of biblical texts and in the historical teachings of Christianity, which they believe require the subordination of women to men.[45] In response to the issues raised by evangelical feminists, a group of conservative Christian leaders met in 1987 in Danvers, Massachusetts, to draw up a statement on gender. That meeting led to the publication of *Recovering Biblical Manhood and Womanhood: A Response to Biblical Feminism*, a book edited by John Piper and Wayne Grudem, which gained tremendous popularity among evangelicals and fundamentalists. It is available in almost any Christian bookstore and was chosen as the book of the year by *Christianity Today* in 1993. Conservative Christians sometimes go so far as to argue that a man should not be placed in a situation subordinate to a woman under any circumstances. They claim that such a situation would invariably violate the essential femininity and masculinity (i.e., the essential nature) of both the woman in authority and the man in subordination.[46] Piper and Grudem put forth this extreme view in their book. An example from my field research illustrates the translation of this ideology from theory to practice. In an interview at a large and well-known Los Angeles church, the assistant pastor indicated that the Piper and Grudem book was one that represented his view. He asserted that not only should women be precluded from church leadership and required to submit to their husbands but that all women in society are to submit to all men in society.

> I would say that . . . there really shouldn't be a different structure for women in society [than there is] in the church. They would need to submit to men in general and they would submit to men in general in the church. Now, if you're going to ask me specific examples, like a woman who teaches a mixed group of high school students, I don't believe that [in our culture] I could ever bring that back, but I don't think that changes the standard.

Though this pastor recognized that his view was not likely to become the reality in modern America, he still believed it was the correct viewpoint, the perspective dictated by God. He went on to explain that the Christian school at his church would not hire a woman as principal,

> because there would be male teachers who would then be required to submit to female leadership, which we believe would be outside the standard of God. . . . In the microcosm of the family, you have two options. If you are a single woman, then you need always to be in the context of submitting yourself to men in general. If you're a married woman, then you need to submit yourself to the authority of your husband.

When pressed to explain how this plays itself out in the day-to-day reality of the church offices, he replied,

> Well, for instance we have a secretarial staff here, some married, some single. We would never put a secretary, or a woman I should say, in charge of a responsibility over a man, even . . . if we had a female secretary and a male secretarial assistant.

"Is that at all practical?" I asked. "Your wife is going to call up a plumber to do a job for her, she's hiring that person, she's in charge." He replied, "Well, actually, what that would be is, it would be my decision . . . and she would simply pursue the function under my leadership." In this interview, I repeatedly pressed the pastor (beyond reason, it seemed to me) to find the point at which he might give in to late-twentieth-century American values of equality. He never did. He remained consistent in his view throughout the interview, pointing to various biblical passages from which he believes his perspective is drawn. I found this surprising because, in most of my interviews, respondents made certain assumptions about me and sought to put their views in the most "positive" light possible. This pastor made no effort to do that, which tipped me off to the reality that this ideological commitment was valuable to him, in part, because it stood in opposition to the culture I represented. No doubt, this assistant pastor was more extreme in his views than most.[47] His church was an influential one, and his views were in keeping with the teachings of his church, the Christian school, the college, and the seminary with which his church was affiliated.

On a popular level, traditionalist gender ideology is also alive and well. Given the growth of the evangelical men's movement Promise Keepers in the 1990s, one could even conclude that this traditionalism is on the upswing. Promise Keepers presents its traditional gender ideology in more palatable language, but the movement is clearly in the traditionalist camp. The fact that Promise Keepers has succeeded in presenting itself as being concerned with encouraging men to be good husbands and fathers, while keeping its very traditional definition of a good husband and father and its gendered notions of godliness well hidden, has many evangelical feminists greatly concerned.[48] Early on, Promise Keepers received much public attention as a result of media interest in its massive gatherings, which were held at sports facilities. Those huge, public campaigns led to the development of small, local "accountability groups" made up of men who had attended the rallies. Promise Keepers grew rapidly through much of the 1990s but then encountered management and financial difficulties that ultimately tempered its influence.[49] By the turn of the century, the very public, well-supported national organization waned in influence, although the smaller local groups have continued to thrive.

Patriarchal theology is not the only perspective to be found among conservative Christians; perhaps surprisingly, there is a variety of feminisms, as well. Evangelical feminists agree that women may be called to all levels of ministry and that marriage is a partnership of equals. Beyond this, there is significant division over other issues including "gender-inclusive God language" and whether homosexuality is to be seen as sin. While many evangelical feminists embrace the practice of modifying all biblical language for gender inclusivity, others use gender-neutral language for humans but resist efforts to change "God language" because they recognize (and choose to maintain) the implicit connection between orthodox theology and patriarchy. One woman pastor, a leader in an evangelical feminist organization, who made this distinction told me:

> I have strong feelings about not using feminine pronouns for God. . . . I use those examples often of places in the Bible where God is referred to in feminine terms. . . . For me the issue of masculine pronouns for God is simply an issue of the Trinity. I just believe that it is the description of the relationship of a father-son, as opposed to father-daughter, mother-daughter. . . . I just feel like that is what God was describing. I don't think it has anything to do with God being masculine at all. . . . I just believe it is a description of the roles.

For example, by "feminine terms" for God this pastor meant passages in which God is described as nurturing. She drew on such passages to develop a perspective of God that included both masculine and feminine, but she stopped short of supporting efforts to change the "father, son, and holy spirit" language of traditional orthodoxy to terms like "creator, redeemer, and sustainer."

Many biblical feminist works begin with a statement in support of the infallibility and complete authority of the Bible. They use conservative hermeneutical methods, with a preference for literal interpretation of texts. However, instead of beginning with Paul's comments on women's roles and their relationships to men, biblical feminists begin with verses like Galatians 3:28 ("there is no male or female in Christ") and interpret other passages through this lens. They conclude that, rightly interpreted, the Bible commands gender equality. Discussion in these works often focuses on the notion of "headship," since the antifeminists argue that the Bible is clear in making husbands "heads" over their wives.[50] What did Paul mean when he argued that the man was the "head" of the woman? Biblical feminists go to the original Greek and argue that the word *kephale,* which is translated as "head," does not include the idea of "authority over" as it does in English. Had Paul wanted to denote "authority over," he would have used another term. They contend that *kephale* means head as in "source" (the head of a river, for example) and argue that Paul is referring to the creation account in which man was created first. They then cite Paul's later statement that, although woman originally came from man, through the birthing process all men come from women. They conclude that if one views these passages in light of Paul's statement in Galatians that there "is no male or female in Christ," the Bible necessarily teaches equality between men and women. The proper relationship between husbands and wives, for the biblical feminists, is "mutual submission." They point out that the passage in Ephesians (5:21–33) that commands wives to submit to their husbands is immediately preceeded by a command that all Christians submit to one another. "Does Paul's command that husbands love their wives," they ask, "not include an assumption that wives should also love their husbands?"

On the issue of women in leadership in religious institutions, biblical feminists again argue that traditionalists misinterpret the relevant texts. Paul may indeed have commanded women to be silent in church, but he seems to undermine an interpretation that would apply this to all Christians in all contexts when, a few short verses later, he describes the proper manner in which women should prophesy (with their heads covered). Biblical feminists prefer the King James translation of 1 Corinthians 13:12, in which Paul says he doesn't permit women to "usurp" authority over men. That does not mean, in their view, that women cannot have authority, merely that they are not to take authority that is not rightly theirs. In fact, they go to great lengths to explain that the Greek word Paul used, *authentein*, is relatively rare and carries with it the notion of grabbing authority illegitimately, in contrast to the more common *exousia*, which means simply "to have authority."

Biblical feminists point out numerous New Testament examples that they believe show women functioning as church leaders with Paul's approval. They believe Phoebe, for example, led a "house church," while Priscilla was commended by Paul for preaching the Gospel and was even given primacy over her husband, Aquila, with whom she preached.

Biblical feminists criticize their theological opponents for "selective literalism," claiming that they themselves are the "true literalists." They point out what they see as inconsistencies that result from their opponents' exegesis of Paul's telling women to be silent and then instructing them in how to speak, for example arguing that, since the Bible cannot contradict itself, the traditionalist exegesis must be wrong. Biblical feminists do not resort to modern culture, a human sense of justice, or allegorization of the text to defend their positions. Instead, they proceed with biblical exegesis in the manner accepted in their subculture. They turn gender theology on its head, but they use the traditional methods to do so.

True to their conservative Protestant heritage, which holds that right behavior follows from correct belief and that ideas have consequences, these biblical feminists have focused most of their efforts on the development and dissemination of Christian feminist thought. There are at least two organizations leading this effort. Christians for Biblical Equality and the Evangelical Women's Caucus are nonprofit research and education organizations that teach biblical feminism. InterVarsity Press has long taken the lead in publishing biblical feminist books. Other evangelical publishing houses, including Baker, Thomas Nelson, and Eerdmans, have also published such works. One of the earliest expositions of this perspective, entitled *God's Word to Women,* by Katherine Bushnell, was published in 1919;[51] it is still in print and is distributed (in bulk) by Christians for Biblical Equality.

An important indicator of the influence of this movement is the presence of biblical feminist ideas at Fuller Theological Seminary. Fuller is the largest interdenominational evangelical seminary in the world. Initially taking a conservative view on questions about appropriate roles for women, the school found itself embroiled in controversy when in 1975, the theology professor Paul Jewett published his controversial defense of women's equality in MAN as Male and Female.[52] Since that time, Fuller has adopted a policy of hiring only teachers who are committed to women's ordination. Evangelical feminist understandings of biblical passages are taught in classes, and Fuller has endorsed a strong statement in support of gender-inclusive language, requiring that all written work turned in by students make use of such language. But even at Fuller Seminary, tensions and conflict over gender persist. And, at other evangelical institutions, the growing evangelical feminist presence is producing major battles.

Creative Blending

While elites formulate (and fight over) conservative Christian gender ideology, members of the subculture mold it and shape it depending on their own circumstances. Examples from my field research in conservative Christian churches in Los Angeles illustrate well some of the ways in which these gender norms are constructed individually, varying with the specific set of circumstances.[53] Sometimes the result is a creative blending of traditionalism and feminism, often by Christians who feel no need to choose between the two.[54]

The first example is drawn from an inner-city fundamentalist church. Although the church leadership is primarily white, the congregation itself is ethnically diverse, and services are conducted in English with Spanish translation. According to the pastor, and in keeping with my own observations, the congregation is 30 percent Latino/a, 20 percent African American, and 25 percent Asian (the ethnic-racial makeup of the remaining 25 percent was not readily evident.) The pastor proudly claims the label "fundamentalist." Distancing himself from evangelicals, he rejects that label altogether and blames evangelicals, not liberals, for the evils of modern society. This particular church holds to a stringent understanding of prescribed gender roles. Women are not permitted leadership roles in the church. They are to submit to their husbands, who are responsible for leading their families. In one of my interviews, a newly wed husband told me that he had recently put these principles into practice in his own family by taking sole responsibility for managing the family finances. His wife no longer had access to their checking account. Under the new system, she came to him and told him how much money she needed and for what purpose; he decided whether the expenditure was necessary and gave her what he thought she needed. Church members can study up on "what the Bible teaches" about men and women and their respective roles with materials available for purchase in the church bookstore. Bookstore shelves hold an extensive collection of books by the fundamentalist John R. Rice, including his antifeminist work *Bobbed Hair, Bossy Wives, and Women Preachers*.[55] The title of this book serves to sum up the position of the congregation on questions about proper roles for women.

But what happens to this ideology in practice? Upon entering the church building, a visitor sees several collections of photographs of church leaders. Since many of the photographs are of couples, one might assume that they depict elders and their wives, deacons and their wives, and so forth. Yet, when asked who these people are, the pastor responded, "They are our stewards." I asked what stewards did and whether both men and women could be stewards. The pastor replied that they ran the classes that were taught (to adults) at the church and that, yes, women were stewards. When pushed on how that jibed with his interpretation of certain Bible passages prohibiting women from teaching men, he informed me that they did not actually teach; they merely ran audiotape machines on which teachings were played.

This explanation sufficed only until I interviewed one of those female stewards. When asked how she understood her role, she told me that she ran "class meetings." When I asked whether that conflicted with Paul's teachings on appropriate roles for women, she demurred, reminding me that she was "still in Bible College," and added that she expected to teach when she was finished.

> I think that it's important to do all that you can. And the Bible teaches that a woman is not supposed to be put in authority over a man and feel like "I'm the head of this house," per se. But in a teaching environment you're not doing that. You're just presenting what's in the Bible in the sense that you're trying to help somebody. And I don't think there's anything [wrong with that].

When I pointed out that Paul said that women weren't to teach men and asked whether that caused tension for her, she gave me a most interesting reply.

No. Because I'd have to spend some time looking at that. That Greek word—I've found that words usually have a lot of different meanings and different applications, you know, back then. And he may have meant I don't want her to teach in the sense that she's telling men what to do, basically. But as far as teaching somebody how to—you know, I'm teaching you how to do this particular job. Which, if I'm teaching you how to win souls for Christ, I'm teaching you. "This is how you do this—" I think that's okay.

When talking about the relationship between husbands and wives, this church steward also took leave of the teachings of her church. I asked her to talk about what submission meant in the context of a marriage relationship, and she replied,

> To me it means if your husband says something—just say for instance, you are in the room and your child is there and your husband tells your child to do something—instead of saying, "honey I don't think that's right" in front of the child, it means hold your tongue until the child is in the other room. And then in a low voice, without disrespecting your husband, you state what you think.

I persisted and asked her whether her husband should do the same if she had done something with which he disagreed. She replied that, yes, he should. This steward had redefined submission as something that both partners owe mutually to each other. Hers were textbook "biblical feminist" responses, though she had obviously not heard the ideas from the pulpit. Her evangelical tradition, which supports the idea that each person is capable of interpreting the Bible for himself or herself, might have lent legitimacy to her difference of opinion with the pastor. At any rate, the discontinuity between what she had heard from the pulpit and her own decisions about her roles seemed not to bother her in the least.

In another traditionalist church, many of the families home-school their children. Although the church teaches sharply delineated gender roles, when I interviewed the mother in one of the families in the church, I noted the subtle ways in which home-schooling activities play a role in shaping the gender identities of these fundamentalists, often in opposition to the ideals held up by their church. Mothers are urged to be homemakers rather than professionals and yet find themselves modeling the professionalization of teaching. The woman I interviewed had attended training programs for home schoolers and read extensively about teaching methods. Women are frequently responsible for choosing the subjects to be studied and designing the curriculum to be used; they become professional teachers. As Colleen McDannell has argued,

> Being the sole provider for their children's education not only increases the mother's responsibility, it gives her a respectable career. . . . They put together weekly lesson plans, survey the variety of academic curricula available, and attend summer teaching seminars. Teaching becomes their profession. . . . They have found an occupation that is fully acceptable within their religious and cultural milieu and that also places them within the wider profession of educators.[56]

For their part, fathers find that their "traditional family values" require that they play a much greater role in the lives of their children than the patriarchal ideal might suggest. In a phenomenon also noted in Orthodox Jewish homes by Lynn Davidman in *Tradition in a Rootless World*, fundamentalist Christian home schools provide an example of the ways in which fundamentalist fathers are encouraged to play a more active role in the domestic lives of their families by participating and doing some of the teaching themselves.[57]

Moreover, this creative blending is more than merely the failure of people to live up to their ideals or the accommodation of one set of ideals to another. It draws on different values and ways of ordering reality in our complex world. This kind of blending indicates a willingness to see an ideal as tentative and an openness to criticism and improvement, even when such criticism and improvement might come from "outside."

The subtle blending of traditionalism and feminism occurs not only in practice but even at the rhetorical level. Susan Harding, in her study of the rhetoric of Jerry Falwell, discusses a sermon in which Falwell jokes about reducing marital discord by "surrendering" to his wife.

> In twenty-eight years we've had some knock-downs and drag-outs. I've lost every one of them. I tell you, men, the best thing you can do is quickly raise your hands and unconditionally surrender because you're gonna lose.[58]

Harding explains that what Falwell has done here is to smooth over the literal reading of "God's chain of command." The joke, she argues, has the qualities of an open secret, of speaking in code, at once displaying and concealing things everyone was dimly aware of but never discussed . . . [it] signaled tension and flux in realm of public male authority.[59]

While conservative Christians may see feminism as a serious threat to "the family," they may at the same time recognize that feminists are right when they say that men have been too easily excused from the responsibility to provide their families with more than just money. Feminists may recognize that there is something to the criticism that they may have been so focused on securing career opportunities for women that they have all but said that choosing motherhood as a career is a copout. Neither group is likely to acknowledge that those criticisms by their opponents have impacted their way of looking at things, but the influence seems clear.

Chapter Outline

The first part of this book, "War Stories," consists of three chapters that explore the parameters and dimensions of gender conflict at institutional and individual levels through case studies. Chapter 1 explores the rise of evangelical feminism during the 1970s and 1980s through the story of one of the key organizations promoting this view, Christians for Biblical Equality (CBE). Across the board, women who managed to weather the storms of controversy agreed that good mentoring and a network of support were the most significant factors in their being able to do so. A central function of biblical feminist organizations is the effort to provide networks that members describe as invaluable lifelines. In addition to its emphasis on helping women to develop support networks, CBE is one of the groups in the forefront of promoting biblical feminism. As CBE challenges a key point in the dominant ideology of the fundamentalist movement, it must, at the same time, work to maintain its position within that subculture. This chapter explores the methods by which it does so.

Chapter 2 looks at a specific conflict over gender as a case study. As organizations like Christians for Biblical Equality began to influence the conservative Christian subculture, those who held views on the roles of women that CBE sought to challenge began to fight back. In the summer of 1998, the Southern Baptist Convention created public controversy when it passed a resolution calling for women's submission. This public statement was the culmination of two decades of fundamentalist efforts to regain control of their denomination and to "return it to its biblical roots." Over these two decades, "right views on women" replaced belief in inerrancy as the measuring stick by which fundamentalists judged orthodoxy. Early on, as conservatives took control of the seminaries, they instituted a requirement that all faculty members sign an inerrancy statement. But as they gained strength, the test became more stringent and faculty members were required to endorse a conservative gender statement. This chapter traces the development of that test of orthodoxy at Southern Seminary, the Southern Baptist flagship seminary, and focuses on the turning point in which the centrality of gender to the subculture identity was solidified by the Southern Baptist leadership.

As various factions vie to gain the ascendancy in the struggle over which will hold the power to interpret gender, and thereby to mold the subculture to their own liking, they create turmoil and conflict in the personal, professional, and spiritual lives of individual women. Having set the stage by looking at institutional conflict in Chapters 1 and 2, in Chapter 3 we look at the impact of this conflict on the lives of individual women in two different contexts: women in pastoral ministry and women in Christian higher education. These contexts were chosen because they are central to the perpetuation and replication of the culture. Women in pastoral ministry and in Christian higher education face the gender-related conflict more often than women in other fundamentalist contexts. They report being frequently challenged regarding the legitimacy of their serving in the positions they hold and therefore must regularly defend themselves. This chapter focuses on individual stories and the common themes that arise from them. It discusses, for example, the double-bind in which women's full professional development is dependent upon their modeling "good Christian character," an aspect of which they must demonstrate by effectively executing traditional family roles. Women are at a disadvantage in this system because family responsibilities fall most heavily on them, although little to no accommodation is made for this fact. I present the stories of women pastors whose husbands were ridiculed for allowing them to take on those roles; of a woman professor who was hired and then, after moving her residence and beginning the school year, dismissed because the board decided it didn't want women as professors; and of women college students at religious institutions who were taken to task for "being feminists" by fellow students and, on at least one occasion, even by a professor in class.

In Part II, "Analysis and Interpretation," we bring critical analysis and theoretical reflection to bear on the material presented in the case studies. Chapter 4 lays out the relevant theoretical perspectives concerning the significance of conflict in understanding culture. It draws on the analysis of conflict in the work of Chidester and Linenthal, Hunter and Wuthnow, exploring the processes by which culture (specifically religious culture) is developed and perpetuated. Raising questions about the meaning of gender for conservative Christians, this chapter critiques existing analyses of conservative Christian gender culture that merely reproduce the traditionalist view that submission is actually empowering. It looks at the conflict between traditionalists and feminists over the true reading of history in regards to Christian views on gender.

Chapter 5 examines the methods by which the traditionalist gender culture of conservative Christians is created, replicated, and fought for. It explores gender-related behavior codes and material culture (the significance of the seemingly insignificant) and their roles in maintaining the gender ideology. It argues that institutional aspects of conservative Protestantism effectively freeze women out of positions of power and authority even within those organizations that ostensibly promote women to leadership. It looks at gender norms and expectations as key cultural markers and boundary-setting devices, as well as the influence of the conservative Christian patriarchal model of the family on relations among Christians and the impact of that model on fostering the gender conflicts and difficulties explored in Part I.

Chapter 6 examines the lives of the women caught in conflict to answer the question, What do we now know about conservative Protestant women in leadership that was obscured when we ignored the stories of conflict? In addition to their reliance on support networks, most women agreed that when they successfully navigated a conflict, their success had as much to do with style as it did any concrete action they had taken. We explore those elements of style, how they work and what they cost. This chapter also compares generational differences in conflict management styles, and the ways in which, for some, the conflicts punctuate their journeys out of evangelicalism.

The conclusion begins by asking why gender is of such importance in the fundamentalist subculture that it has become the core issue in defining fundamentalist identity. It draws on concrete examples from the interview data to look at the various cultural aspects of fundamentalist gender ideology and practice. I argue that conservative Christian gender ideology symbolizes and embodies a cosmic dualism that gives meaning, order, and purpose to the universe. The dualism replicates the traditional Christian dichotomy between the sacred and the profane, the Creator and the creation, good and evil. For antifeminist fundamentalists, undermining the clear-cut divisions between masculinity and femininity is threatening because it undermines the very order of the universe itself.

My students often comment that people should not try to change religious institutions, that if they are unhappy with how things are, they should go elsewhere. My conclusion ties together the material presented in the previous chapters and brings it to bear on exactly this issue. The premise of this book is that religious traditions are cultural systems that are always in a process of change, that they do not exist in some pure form apart from a culture and never have. The question then becomes not whether people should bring change but who will decide how the inevitably transformed tradition will look—what will be the processes by which change occurs, what will be the costs of that change, and to whom will those costs accrue?

whether people should bring change but who will decide how the m

PART I

War Stories

*Case Studies in Gender Conflict in Institutions
and in the Lives of Individuals*

Christians for Biblical Equality and the Fight for Middle Ground

I interviewed Nikki, a professor at a well-known conservative seminary, at a Christians for Biblical Equality conference. She told me of the problems she had encountered in her position at the seminary and also shared stories about coworkers and students. She then described how CBE functioned as the core of women's support networks, helping them adapt their theology to make sense of what they believed to be true in a manner that allowed them to maintain their faith commitments.

> The CBE becomes their place to go where they are going to be loved. They are accepted. They are with it scripturally, not a heretic. And this is where the strength comes from here and why we have to be here. For those of us who are really in the fundamentalist thing there is tremendous fear of losing our scriptural foundations because we are so afraid of what will happen to us spiritually. . . . There is still [at CBE] this sense that the Scripture is the whole counsel of God. You don't ignore any part of it because you don't happen to agree with it but you look at it in the wholeness of it rather than in bits and pieces. . . . It's the one place I know where I can express my heart toward God and my desire for what I would like to do and what I would like to see the church look like and not be laughed at or have a Bible verse thrown in my face. It's a place where I can come and affirm the femininity as well as the masculinity of God and not be told I am a heretic.

She explained how CBE strengthened her and gave her a vision of how she could stay within the conservative Christian world and make a difference.

There was this woman [who spoke] last night. She's a professional ac-
countant and [she and her husband] moved seven or eight months ago
and they've been trying to find a church ever since they moved there.
[The town they moved to] is the center of the right-wing Christian movement and all of the churches there are pastored by graduates [of the seminary where I teach]. It's for women like her that I keep thinking, if I stay
[in my job] and influence ten or twelve or twenty students that graduate
every year or two to be more affirming and accepting, then I'm really having a magnificent ministry.

During the 1970s and 1980s, a significant feminist movement developed
among conservative American Protestants and at a number of organizations that promoted "biblical feminism"; related viewpoints gained support in many key institutions. The growing belief that the Bible commands gender equality produced a generation of conservative Christian
women who expected opportunities they ultimately did not find. Christians for Biblical Equality (CBE) was one of the groups in the forefront of
promoting biblical feminism, challenging a key point in the dominant ideology of the evangelical subculture and at the same time working to retain
its position within that subculture.[1] The fact that CBE members are educated (graduate degrees are common), white, and middle class significantly influenced the form and activities of this movement, which consist
almost exclusively of publications and conferences.[2] CBE has two primary
goals: to educate conservative Christians about the "truth" concerning
women and women's equality according to the Bible and to maintain the
legitimacy of its place within the larger evangelical subculture so that it
can effectively pursue the first goal.[3]

Biblical Feminism: Is CBE Really Feminist?

Evangelical Christians who call themselves feminists are not readily accepted by the larger feminist movement as ideological kin. Since there
is no single definition of "feminist," assessing the legitimacy of CBE's
use of the term is more difficult than it might seem. In defense of its
use of the label, CBE cites *Webster's New Collegiate* Dictionary: "Feminism is the theory of the political, economic, and social equality of the
sexes [or] organized activity on behalf of women's rights and interests."[4]

CBE describes itself as "an organization of Christians who believe that the Bible, properly interpreted, teaches the fundamental equality of men and women." It thus sees itself as rightful heir to the nineteenth-century women's rights movement.[5]

Biblical feminists believe that church leadership and pastoral roles should not be denied to women, that the ideal for a marriage relationship is "mutual submission," and that a just society will not use gender as a reason for limiting the roles a person may play: "any limitation or denial of the human rights of women cannot be reconciled with Christ's clear call to take up our cross and follow him."[6] For the most part, CBE promotes the use of inclusive language in the church, although there is still some reluctance to change "God language."[7]

But some secular and religious feminists outside this evangelical movement take issue with the limited, narrow dictionary definition of feminism embraced by CBE. Many of them believe that a commitment to feminism includes more than support for functional equality between men and women; for these feminists, feminism is a deeper critique that seeks reform of underlying patriarchal structures that shape perspectives and attitudes about women.

Catherine Kroeger and the Founding of CBE

Catherine Kroeger believes that she has a mission from God. At more than seventy years of age, she still gets up before daybreak to make the two-hour drive from her home in Brewster, Massachusetts, to Gordon Seminary, where she teaches Greek. Kroeger has felt called to some kind of professional Christian service at least since she was a seventeen-year-old college student. She described those years as ones in which she struggled to discern what God would have her do with her life: "I tried to pass over the difficult biblical passages for a time, but they eventually caught up with me," she said.

She continued, "As a student at Bryn Mawr College during World War II, I asked A. J. Gordon's daughter Harriet[8] about women in the Bible, and she gave me a copy of Katherine Bushnell's *God's Word to Women*."[9] Kroeger had studied some Greek and believed it was enough to "check on Bushnell's argument." " I found it a bit extreme," she told me, "so I put it away, but every year or so something would happen and I'd bring it out." Paraphrasing Bushnell, Kroeger said,

> Until we get people to deal with all of this [the 'difficult' passages], women will be given over to fashion and folly. "Where are our women interpreters?" I asked. But I'm going to be a missionary to Saudi Arabia, I sure hope God works it out.

But, due to health problems, Kroeger never made it to the foreign mission field. Her concern about women and what God wants for them led her to find her own mission field among women in conservative churches here in the United States.

Like many of the women I interviewed, for years Kroeger believed that she was alone in her views. When she attended the Washington meeting of the Evangelical Women's Caucus (EWC), in 1975, she was "thrilled to find so many women with these same ideas." My respondents each echoed this sentiment. They compared their discovery of the biblical feminist movement to finding home after being lost for years; the terms they use are quite like terms used to describe a conversion experience. Feeling alienated from the rest of Christendom, many of those involved found a surrogate church and family among their evangelical feminist sisters.

Kroeger's vision, which was shared by many from the beginning, was for the biblical feminist movement to serve as a feminist outreach to women in conservative churches. Many of the early supporters had come from such churches and knew firsthand the anguish experienced by evangelical/fundamentalist women who had made "nontraditional" choices (or who longed to do so). According to Kroeger and to the women I interviewed at the CBE conference, many of them needed "solid biblical exegesis" to reconcile their conservative faith with their feminist sensibilities, and they recognized that they were unlikely to find a home in more secular feminism.

Kroeger was heavily involved in the EWC from that 1975 meeting on. She believes, in hindsight, that there were divisions from the beginning (particularly over the issue of homosexuality) that would eventually prove to be insurmountable. Kroeger told me, "people kept asking me what did I really think [about the lesbian presence]. I was increasingly troubled, but kept telling myself, 'you can't have everything.'"

In 1986, the question of homosexuality was brought to a head when the Evangelical Women's Caucus voted in favor of the following resolution supporting civil rights for homosexuals:

Whereas homosexual people are children of God, and because of the biblical mandate of Jesus Christ that we are all created equal in God's sight, and in recognition of the lesbian minority in the Evangelical Women's Caucus International, EWC takes a firm stand in favor of civil rights protection for homosexual persons.[10]

Opposition from many of the more conservative feminists stemmed, at least in part, from a genuine concern for the implications of embracing this particular civil rights issue for the mission of the organization. Many believed that identification with gay and lesbian rights would decimate any hope of influencing evangelicalism on the question of the roles of women. Furthermore, many of the women in EWC were in delicate positions as leaders in conservative churches or as teachers at evangelical colleges. They were painfully aware of the precariousness of their positions, and many had already faced difficulties because of their embrace of feminism. They feared that for them to identify with an organization that was perceived as endorsing lesbianism might be tantamount to committing professional suicide.[11] One interviewee said it most clearly:

> I did not want the group taking this on as a major issue because I felt like then it would weaken our defense of biblical feminism. And so that's the point that really upset me. I thought it was a major political mistake. I thought it meant the death of EWC, and it has. I mean the organization still survives, but it's not the same organization. . . . People to whom the organization could speak just discredit it.[12]

Many of those conservatives felt the need to distance themselves from EWC and met to discuss the possibility of forming a new organization. Initially the group established itself under the umbrella of a London-based group, Men, Women, and God (MWG). MWG had some instant credibility in evangelical circles because of its association with the London Institute for Contemporary Christianity and with the well-known evangelical theologian John Stott. The international ties, however, proved to be cumbersome, and shortly thereafter, the North American group established its independence and renamed itself Christians for Biblical Equality.[13]

By 1989, CBE had joined the National Association of Evangelicals and boasted a circulation of 1,540 for its quarterly journal, *The Priscilla Papers*. Since its founding, CBE has sponsored a major conference on biblical feminism every other year. The organization produces two regular periodicals, *The Priscilla Papers* and *Mutuality*, publishes and distributes biblical feminist books, and supports various local chapter activities.

Holding the Middle Ground

Since its founding, CBE has walked a thin line between embracing what is seen by many in the subculture as a liberal cause and maintaining the solidity of its position within the evangelical subculture. It has worked to mitigate criticisms that biblical feminism cannot "really be Christian," largely by offering repeated reassurances that permitting women to exercise greater authority, and even to achieve equality with men, will not ultimately alter the foundations of the evangelical worldview.

From the beginning, CBE has relied on the credibility and endorsement of sympathetic "big names" to allay the fears of suspicious evangelicals. In 1990, when CBE took a full-page ad in *Christianity Today* that included a list of illustrious signatories, you could almost hear readers asking, "How bad could it be? I mean, Richard Mouw thinks it's okay." As early as 1986, the support of John Stott was seen as crucial to the survival of the fledgling organization. Through the years, Kroeger actively cultivated a list of well-known supporters (which, according to Kroeger, now has well in excess of two hundred names), knowing the ability of these "stars" to confer credibility. At least one interviewee, who participated in CBE conferences, saw in this tactic the persistence of patriarchal hierarchicalism.

> I think the structure [of CBE] is very male-hierarchical. I think they've just replaced one hierarchical structure with another. . . . I felt like it [the conference] was a cult of celebrities. They made their writers and speakers into specialists, and everybody came to them as if they had the answers to all their questions. . . . I think a feminist organization has to propose an alternative. The board [of CBE] should be consciously nonhierarchical. The speakers and leaders should be presented as everyday people.[14]

This same respondent explained that she thought that CBE's understanding of feminism was different from hers on this point. What she was looking for was a "worldview change—a more women-friendly environment—less focused on celebrities." She argued that "you're not going to be able to include women in general, or empower them, until you change the rules." CBE, on the other hand, had staked out a position that minimized the significance of the changes that would be necessary for women to achieve equality and emphasized the credibility of evangelical celebrities to reassure skeptics.

Biblical feminists are insistent on their credentials as evangelicals by virtue of their "endorsement of, and submission to, biblical authority." The thoughts of a CBE member who pastors a small church in California were representative of many in her answer to my question "What is your view of the Bible?" She said, "I believe the Bible is infallible. I believe everything in the Bible is the revealed word of God. And I believe the Bible includes everything we need to know to understand God and our salvation."[15]

When asked "What about your doctrine of salvation? Must people accept Jesus to be saved?" she answered yes and continued that she believed that Jesus was literally God in human form and that the virgin birth literally happened.

Most biblical feminist books begin with some sort of disclaimer to this effect. Even the most outspoken opponents of biblical feminism, John Piper and Wayne Grudem, acknowledge biblical feminists' claim to this most important of evangelical credentials:

> These authors differ from secular feminists because they do not reject the Bible's authority or truthfulness, but rather give *new interpretations* of the Bible to support their claims. We may call them "evangelical feminists" because by personal commitment to Jesus Christ and by profession of belief in the total truthfulness of Scripture they still identify themselves clearly with evangelicalism. Their arguments have been detailed, earnest, and pervasive to many Christians.[16] (italics in original)

The style of exegesis employed by evangelical feminists is also in keeping with the style approved in the larger community of evangelical believers. Arguments over the best translation of the Greek and Hebrew texts are ongoing, as illustrated by the previously discussed example of the interpretation of the Greek word *kephale*. This level of engagement over technical meanings of individual words to ascertain the "original intent" of the sacred text is clearly in keeping with the evangelical tradition. Entire books are devoted to debates over the interpretation of certain texts.[17]

Biblical feminists work diligently to reclaim the history of the evangelical movement and even the history of Christianity itself. They argue that antifeminism is recent and, in fact, itself an accommodation to the culture of the 1950s.[18] In the face of talk about "traditional family values," biblical feminists point to Margaret Fell's 1667 argument for women's right to speak in public[19]; to the involvement of nineteenth-century evangelical women in the movements for abolition, temperance, and women suffrage; to the activities of women evangelists and missionaries; and to Katherine Bushnell's work in 1912. The fall 1992 issue of *The Priscilla Papers* included an article on the degree to which turn-of-the-century fundamentalists and holiness churches supported, trained, and encouraged women missionaries. A later issue contained an article on nineteenth-century women hymn writers.[20] CBE's 1995 catalog includes several books about women mentioned in the Bible (which they see as the historical record, including women's history); an entire section is headed "Women in the History of the Church." CBE even sells photocopies of Janette Hassey's out-of-print *No Time for Silence*, which, as the promotional note for the book illustrates, fosters this goal of reclaiming history. The note describes Hassey's book as

> An historical examination of the ministry of women in evangelical groups and denominations between 1880 and 1930. Shows that groups formerly welcoming and affirming women in the ministry often now oppose them, not understanding their own history.[21]

Through the promotion and distribution of these works, evangelical feminists endeavor to show that so-called traditional evangelical attitudes toward women and women's leadership are actually relatively new and that women have always served God in public roles. They are thus calling the church back to what they see as the truth and away from its imposition of more limited roles for women, which they view as a modern innovation.

Biblical feminists also attempt to safeguard their position as evangelicals by supporting the behavioral codes and notions of purity that predominate in the larger evangelical world, aligning themselves with socially conservative evangelicals. An interview with a pastor, a member of CBE, drove home the importance of this alignment for maintaining this moral legitimacy:

> Some people [in a church considering hiring her as their pastor] were afraid that if I was a pastor I would be against marriage and kids and hav-

ing a family. But they knew I had a good marriage. I had great kids. So even though some people said that, they already knew it wasn't true.[22]

In another example of this endorsement of traditional Christian morality, an issue of *The Priscilla Papers* that was devoted to singleness included an article entitled "Sexual Infidelity as Exploitation," which equated premarital sex with infidelity.[23] Perhaps the clearest example of this assent to traditional evangelical morality is CBE's statement of faith, which begins by acknowledging the authority of the Bible and concludes with the following statement, which grew out of the earlier conflict over gay and lesbian rights: "We believe in the family, celibate singleness, and faithful heterosexual marriage as the patterns God has designed for us."[24] In one fell swoop, CBE shows that, with the exception of the submission of women to men, it is basically supportive of the "pro-family" views of evangelicals. This point in the statement of faith is one to which all evangelicals, whether or not they are sympathetic to feminism, could give assent.

One CBE conference package contained a listing of the conference speakers and provided biographical information for each. Showing that biblical feminists are not a threat to the family, most of the introductions concluded with the name of the speaker's spouse and the number of children the couple had; none said that the speaker was single or divorced. Being married and having children is clearly still a badge of honor in this world, but it's also an indication that the person is "safe" and does not represent a threat to the moral order of the community.

Another example in which the biblical feminists maintain and support the broader moral order of the subculture has to do with the use of alcohol. While abstinence is neither officially required nor endorsed by CBE, Cathy Kroeger has conservative, traditionally evangelical views on the consumption of alcohol. No alcohol is permitted in her home, and she told me that she had been surprised and dismayed to find that alcohol was available at an informal get-together at an Evangelical Women's Caucus meeting a few years prior.

Antifeminist evangelicals have charged that feminists are in league with those who would promote moral laxity and sexual license. Biblical feminists have set out to differentiate themselves from the larger culture on these issues and to align themselves with other conservative Christians. This is nowhere more clear than it is concerning the issue of homosexuality. It was the apparent endorsement of lesbianism by the EWC that prompted the formation of CBE. Kroeger told me that there were many points on which she disagreed with other EWC leaders but that the resolution in favor of civil rights for homosexuals was the one that couldn't be ignored.

The clause in specific support of heterosexuality in CBE's statement of faith is a direct result of this controversy. For the first few years, CBE avoided the issue in publications and at conference workshops. One conference did engage the topic in a workshop entitled "The Challenges of Homosexuality: Speaking the Truth in Love," but clearly the position taken was a "safe" one within the subculture.

CBE members are emphatic that, while homosexuals are deserving of Christian love, the practice of homosexuality is unequivocally sinful. One biblical feminist respondent who has remained a member of EWC and supported the gay and lesbian rights resolution articulated the position clearly:

> I don't want to judge people, women who choose to live together, and I would like to be their friend. I like to just not have a judgmental spirit toward them even though I don't believe that's the way human kind was intended to function. . . . I guess you could say I'm heterosexist. I have good friends who are lesbians and I don't feel like it's my place to judge. I can't get around what it seems to be Scripture clearly teaches about same-sex relationships. I don't think you can get around it without really twisting Scripture a lot.[25]

Homosexuality is unrivaled as a hot-button issue among conservative evangelicals and fundamentalists.[26] It is particularly problematic for biblical feminists who wish to retain a claim to evangelical orthodoxy. In the larger feminist movement, gay rights and women's rights have been inextricably linked. And, even in the evangelical world, the interpretation of texts used by biblical feminists is often also used to defend homosexuality.

This point has not been missed by the "traditionalist" opponents of biblical feminism. Evangelical opponents of biblical feminism charge that biblical feminists believe that, aside from biological differences, men and women are exactly the same and that nonbiological gendered differences are all cultural.[27] Like secular feminists, biblical feminists disagree over this question, but the fact remains that there is a pervasive concern that equality for women (as defined by feminists) will result in an increased incidence of homosexuality and will leave no grounds from which to oppose homosexuality. This concern is apparent in the most significant recent antifeminist work, Piper and Grudem's *Recovering Biblical Manhood and Womanhood: A Response to Evangelical Feminism:*

> To us it is increasingly and painfully clear that biblical feminism is an unwitting partner in unraveling the fabric of complementary manhood and womanhood that provides the foundation for biblical marriage and biblical church order, but also for heterosexuality as well.[28] The effort of contemporary society to eradicate the differences between the sexes has spawned an increase in strident lesbianism and open homosexuality, a quantum leap in divorces, an increase in rapes and sexual crimes of all sorts—and families smaller in size than ever before.[29]

In reference to Paul Jewett's work *MAN as Male and Female,*[30] Piper and Grudem write: "If [Galatians literally means] there is no male or female in Christ [as Jewett wants to understand it], how will he [Jewett] oppose homosexuality?"[31] The assumption is that an inability to oppose homosexuality in and of itself proves Jewett's exegesis regarding men and women incorrect.

Those who formed CBE believed that they had to distance themselves from any endorsement of homosexuality if they were to maintain their middle ground between feminism and conservative Protestantism. They believed that there were many evangelicals who might be open to differing views on the roles of women but who would never accept even the hint of support for homosexuality. If evangelicals were to accept their argument that Christianity requires equality for women, biblical feminists themselves had to be above reproach with regard to issues of "purity and morality." They clearly see, though, that their hold on this middle ground is precarious, and they continue to offer constant reassurance that biblical feminism need not undermine the family, heterosexuality, marriage, children, and the like. They pledge their evangelical orthodoxy by maintaining a high view of the authority of the Bible and by claiming the support of evangelical leaders, both past and present. By siding with the larger evangelical subculture on these issues, biblical feminists not only set up their version of feminism as morally acceptable but also created a situation in which they could claim common enemies in the larger culture (although they have never attacked those enemies the way some in the larger evangelical subculture have). In doing so, they have preserved the evangelical demarcation between "us" and "them" and thereby solidified biblical feminists' position on the "us" side with evangelicals. With their loyalty, they buy the power to participate in the production of the dimension of culture they most care about: gender ideology.

Living in the Middle

Maintaining the middle ground is not easy. Many in this movement have lived through experiences that they might describe as being torn limb from limb. One early supporter was dismissed from his position with a major evangelical publisher because of to his support for, and his wife's publication defending, biblical feminism. Men and women have left seminary teaching positions over the issue of women's place in ministry. A woman who taught at another conservative evangelical seminary told me she was agonizing over whether she could remain there, given her views. The situation in which she found herself was so stressful and difficult that she was in therapy and on antidepressants. I interviewed women pastors who keep their CBE membership secret for fear of repercussions in their churches or denominations. One woman told me,

> When I come to CBE I'm home spiritually. It is the one place I'm at home. For years I was just a closet member; I couldn't tell anybody I was part of it. I lived for *The Priscilla Papers*, because four times a year I could read something that would confirm in me that I was not a heretic and I was not headed straight for eternal damnation, that I was still well within the confines of evangelical belief. And yet, where was I going to get my understanding that women are created in the image of God confirmed by scholars? And I really needed it because I couldn't find it anywhere [else].

Another woman, an author of a recent book that puts forth a moderate version of biblical feminism, struggled over whether to use her real name on the cover out of concern for the implications for her husband's career in the subculture.[32]

In interviews with students on several evangelical college campuses, I found that many of them call feminism "the f-word." In surveys at one West Coast and one East Coast school, I found only an insignificant number who had heard of biblical feminism, evangelical feminism, Christian feminism, CBE, or EWC. The few students in the "middle ground" on these campuses reported that they had been berated by fellow students after being seen reading biblical feminist books.[33]

This tension with the larger subculture contributes to the overwhelming joy described by biblical feminists when they find a group like CBE that serves as a surrogate family, an alternative church community, a professional network, and a locus for group therapy. One woman I interviewed at a CBE conference told me,

> Here at the CBE conference there is enormous hurt in the air. I mean, I am sensing it, you look at people's faces and there is a lot of anguish on them. This is not one of those conferences where people are coming to it because they are excited about what they are doing. They are coming for healing here because they're fighting so many battles where they are coming from—many of them are seminary graduates and their heart is in serving their churches, and they can't be ordained, they can't serve communion, they can't even usher, they can't find a church that welcomes them.

Interviewing nearly a decade after the split between the Evangelical Women's Caucus and the Christians for Biblical Equality, I found women still so pained by the event that they had difficulty talking about it. This response makes sense only when we take into account the centrality of this community to these women. Whether they maintained their association with one or both of the factions, the women viewed these groups as refuges from the larger subculture, which they felt undermined their value as human beings.

Prior to the split between EWC and CBE, at least two divergent feminisms were developing. Conservative members saw feminism as a fight for equality between men and women and for justice (narrowly defined) on specific issues such as what opportunities would be open to women in the church and in society at large. At the same time, other members were developing an understanding of sexism as a pervasive social problem (related to racism, militarism, and other forms of oppression) that had to be addressed by a challenge to the patriarchal system that undergirds society. Incorporating the fight for lesbian and gay rights, therefore, was, for them, integral, rather than peripheral.[34] Conservatives held fast to their more narrow focus, avoiding what they saw as detractions from their fight to secure functional equality for women in the church and in the family; a significant part of the traditionalist opposition to women's equality is based on their fear that to accept women as equals would set them on a slippery slope that would ultimately lead to acceptance of homosexuality. Leaders of CBE chose to address this challenge by attempting to extricate their corner of the women's movement from the broader movement against the litany of social evils that are of concern to the subculture. As they did so, the two visions of feminism were increasingly at odds with each other.

Despite divisions within the biblical feminist movement, CBE was relatively successful in promoting its agenda regarding the roles of women in the larger conservative Christian world. It has been particularly successful in influencing major fundamentalist and evangelical institutions. In the 1980s, I was a student at Fuller Theological Seminary, where there was broad-based support for women's equality. Fuller had hosted a conference of the biblical feminist organization Evangelical Women's Caucus (before its split into two factions). There was an active chapter of EWC on campus, all faculty supported women's ordination, and there was an institutional policy requiring that students use gender-inclusive language in their coursework. Fuller was one of many seminaries influenced in this way. *Christianity Today* also regularly presents biblical feminist views and issues and has done so for some time. Even the "Christian Men's Movement" group Promise Keepers has been described as promoting "soft patriarchy" in that it argues for male headship but does so in a way that seems to reflect the softening influence of biblical feminist views and arguments.

The growing influence of biblical feminism is not unchallenged, however. In the next chapter we explore the ways in which leaders in one denomination took control of their seminary to reverse the impact of those who were fighting for changes in the roles of women.

2

Institutional Conflict and the New Orthodoxy at Southern Seminary

In June 2000, the Southern Baptist Convention (SBC) met in Orlando, Florida, and overwhelmingly voted against having women serve as pastors, despite the fact that many women were already serving as pastors in Southern Baptist churches. Specifically, the convention revised the Southern Baptist statement of faith to say that the "office of pastor is limited to men as qualified in Scripture." This move was the culmination of a long-fought battle between moderates and conservatives for control of the nation's largest Protestant denomination. It is also representative of the way in which views on gender issues have become symbolic of the ideological and cultural divide within conservative American Protestantism more generally. Such statements are passed not because they represent the consensus of the organization. Rather, they succeed because they are seen (at least by a powerful faction) as dividing points, as markers that separate the "good guys" from the "bad guys."

When different factions vie for control of a conservative religious institution, gender issues are often buried in other issues. Even where official endorsement of women's secondary status might legitimate discrimination, in most cases those in power have often argued that the "real disagreement" is over theological points such as the inerrancy of the Bible. Those not in power, however, often see gender-related components to the conflicts. This chapter focuses on one major case in which the issues were particularly clear. In the conflict at Southern Baptist Theological Seminary, both sides agreed that gender concerns played a major role in the dispute.

Southern Seminary, in Louisville, Kentucky, provides a good case study for several reasons. First, seminaries are clearly a locus of power within religious denominations, and they control the resources by which religious culture is produced. Second, seminaries bring together the scholars of a religious community, and the collective intellectual life of those scholars constitutes the discourse that becomes the ideological underpinnings to the subculture. Third, seminaries are the training ground for future religious leaders and are, for that reason, vitally important in the reproduction of religious culture. I chose a recent conflict at Southern Seminary as a case study because the fact that the gender lines were made so explicitly clear allows for an examination of the conflict in terms of gender in a way that other situations do not. This particular seminary can be viewed as something of a laboratory in which gender conflict can be fairly clearly isolated from other problems; the ordination of women occupied a central position in the conflict between the two factions seeking to shape the institution.

There are some who would quibble over the description of Southern Baptists as evangelical. The Southern Baptists clearly have their own subculture, one that is distinct from the subculture of other evangelicals. Southern Baptist culture is distinctly Southern, and many Southern Baptists consider evangelicalism to be a "Yankee" phenomenon.[1] This was made graphically clear to me in an interview with Professor Tim Weber, a non-Southern Baptist who had moved from Denver Seminary to Southern Seminary. He explained,

> I was teaching a class on twentieth-century American religion and I talked about David Wells and Richard Mouw and my students just sat there. I said how many of you have heard of these books? How many of you have heard of either of these authors? Nobody. Completely unknown.[2]

Yet, in the larger evangelical culture, these are key figures whose work is widely known.

Perhaps ironically, Southern Baptists seem to conflate the categories "evangelical" and "fundamentalist," considering members of both to be all fundamentalists and all Yankees; evangelicals, on the other hand, often seem to assume that all Southern Baptists are really fundamentalists. To some degree, recent divisions in the SBC can be considered divisions between evangelicals and fundamentalists within the convention, thus illustrating that both can be found there. Nonetheless, scholars have long seen the similarities between Southern Baptists and other evangelicals, refuting the claim made by some Southern Baptists that they do not fit within the fold.[3] Furthermore, the new leadership in the Southern Baptist Convention and at Southern Seminary sees itself as part of the larger evangelical tradition; seminary president R. Albert Mohler uses the label to describe himself and the school.[4] As Weber put it, using the term "evangelical" in a broad way, "there is no other place to put it [the Southern Baptist Convention] with its revivalism and Jesus piety." While in other discussions it may be helpful to think of Southern Baptists as united by a unique subculture that is distinct from that of other conservative Protestants in this country, in this discussion I include them in the broadly inclusive group labeled "evangelicals."[5]

During June 1995, I conducted sixteen formal interviews on the campus of Southern Seminary. I spoke with students, administrators, and tenured faculty members, including the seminary president, R. Albert Mohler; former seminary president Roy Honeycutt; David Dockery, vice president for academic administration and dean of the School of Theology; and Diana Garland, former dean of the School of Social Work. Additionally, I have relied on newspaper clippings, press reports, newsletters, and private correspondence made available to me by some of those I interviewed as primary-source material.[6]

Southern Baptists Divide

In the late 1970s, a group of fundamentalists within the Southern Baptist Convention came to the conclusion that "liberals" had wrested control of several of the most important Baptist agencies and institutions, not the least of which were Southern Baptist institutions of higher education.[7] These fundamentalists realized that if they began electing sympathetic presidents, they could eventually control the various boards and effect a "course correction." Two of the three most often-cited treatments of this controversy in the SBC make little, if any, reference to the role of gender in the dispute. Bill Leonard's *God's Last and Only Hope: The Fragmentation of the Southern Baptist Convention* gives useful cultural context to the "fragmentation" by emphasizing the "southern-ness" of Southern Baptists.[8] Leonard explores the significance of denominationalism and the centrality of doctrine, theology, and popular piety in Southern Baptist life. But, in spite of all the cultural contextualization, in Leonard's treatment the dispute between the fundamentalists and moderates is ultimately over intellectual disagreements.

Nancy Ammerman pays much more attention to the significance of gender issues in her book *Baptist Battles: Social Change and Religious Conflict in the Southern Baptist Convention.* She argues that, even early in the dispute, the question of women's ordination was considered by fundamentalist Southern Baptists to be an indicator of a person's views on biblical inerrancy and theological orthodoxy.[9] But, according to Ammerman, inerrancy was still the central issue; she writes, "Among fundamentalists, the issue at stake in this Baptist battle is very clear: the truth of the Bible."[10] Southern Baptist fundamentalists wished to ensure that Southern Baptist students in Southern Baptist institutions would be educated in a manner consistent with Southern Baptist views that the Bible is the inerrant word of God. The question of women's ordination was relevant in that fundamentalists believed that no inerrantist could support women's ordination and that no one who supported women's ordination could also be inerrantist.[11]

A third treatment of the conflict, the most recent, argues that the point of disagreement between fundamentalists and moderates in the Southern Baptist Convention was not theological or doctrinal. In *Southern Baptist Politics: Authority and Power in the Restructuring of an American Denomination,* Arthur Emery Farnsley II argues that the representatives of the two sides differed, "primarily on their views of polity and policy,"[12] ignoring the significance of gender issues altogether.

Developments at Southern Seminary demonstrate that while fundamentalists and moderates may or may not agree on inerrancy, the dividing line between the two is something deeper. When fundamentalists were able to remove those they perceived as being "on the other side" by challenging them on theological points, they did so. However, once it became clear to the president and trustees of Southern Seminary that there were those who endorsed theological conservatism and biblical inerrancy but were still not "on the team," a new litmus test was introduced that the president and trustees believed more clearly delineated the boundary between themselves and those they perceived as liberals. What was "really" at issue were the larger symbolic values that conflict over gender evokes; gender conflicts now function in the same way that conflict over inerrancy did a generation ago.

The Conflict at Southern

Southern Seminary, often called the flagship Southern Baptist seminary, was not the first of the seminaries to be drawn into a fight between "liberals" and "conservatives," nor was this particular conflict the first to have occurred at Southern.[13]

In 1993, R. Albert Mohler was elected president of Southern Seminary. At thirty-three years old, he was charged with bringing the views promoted by the seminary in line with those of the board of trustees (and, according to the trustees, in line with the views of Southern Baptists). Several controversial resignations followed. Prospective faculty members were scrutinized with regard to their affirmation of the Abstract of Principles, especially its statement on the authority and inerrancy of Scripture. It is quite common for religiously affiliated schools to require assent to a statement of faith from faculty members. The Abstract of Principles, which dates to the founding of the school in 1859 and was authored by Basil Manly Jr., one of the schools' founders, is such a statement.[14] It was in use at other Baptist schools, as well at Southern. In addition to its statement on Scripture, it also takes positions on issues traditionally associated with conservative Christian orthodoxy: the Trinity; the sovereignty of God; salvation by grace through faith; and substitutionary atonement.

In 1991, the faculty, the trustees, and the administration developed a document that became known as the Covenant Renewal, which outlined the responsibilities of each group to the institution. According to Hankins, this document was an effort at compromise between the factions at the seminary and was intended to ensure that new faculty would have a "high view of Scripture."[15] In 1992, five new faculty members were hired under the Covenant Renewal, each of whom affirmed biblical inerrancy. Questions about these new faculty members' views on women's ordination were raised at the time, but their differences with the trustees did not preclude their being hired.[16] Professor Timothy Weber was one of those hired at that time.

I was hired in the spring of '92 when Roy Honeycutt was still president. And he and his provost both assured me that they would be here another five years, that the school had turned a corner, and that to do what it had to do they expected a period of calm and change with structuring. But there seemed to be some kind of plan in operation. In the year that I was hired there were a number of northern evangelical types, Baptists, who were hired to come in.

Weber believed that these northern evangelicals (who were Baptist but not Southern Baptist) were a safe compromise for the board of trustees. They were conservative (all of them "inerrantist" in one way or another), but they had not been part of the fight between the moderates and the fundamentalists in the Southern Baptist convention; "noncombatants," he called them. They were candidates who could be acceptable to both sides.

In February 1995, Southern Seminary announced a search to fill a faculty position in the Carver School of Social Work. A search committee selected David Sherwood, then at Gordon College, as its first choice and made arrangements to bring him to campus. Sherwood was enthusiastically supported at every level of the seminary's hiring process. He met with President Mohler, who indicated his approval pending Sherwood's statements on the Abstract of Principles, on the Covenant Renewal, and his views on "Specified Issues" requested by Mohler.

The questioning of a candidate's views on specific current issues was a new addition to the hiring process. But, a short time later, the trustees endorsed Mohler's addition of this step in the hiring process. Prospective faculty members are now required to articulate conservative views on four "issues of our day," three of which center on gender-related concerns. These issues include abortion, homosexuality, women's ordination, and the uniqueness of the Gospel (i.e., the belief that the only way to salvation is the acceptance of Jesus as savior).

Sherwood affirmed every point of the Abstract of Principles and the Covenant Renewal. He stated his opposition to abortion, his view that all sex outside marriage (which is, by definition in this context, heterosexual) is sinful, and his belief that salvation comes through Jesus alone. In his statement on "The Role of Women in the Ministry of the Church," Sherwood renounced any "androgynous ideal," acknowledged legitimate disagreement on the roles of women among evangelicals committed to the "full authority of Scripture," but argued that "God's spirit blows where it wills and certain (but not all) women may be called to any role in the ministry of the church."[17]

Despite Sherwood's agreement with fundamentalists on every point but the last, Mohler informed Diana Garland, dean of the School of Social Work, that he would not support Sherwood's election to the faculty. Upon learning of this new criterion for hiring, Dean Garland informed President Mohler that she was considering resigning her position as dean because she believed she would not be able to find an acceptable candidate to fill the faculty position. Garland believed the accreditation of the School of Social Work to be in jeopardy because it had an insufficient number of tenured faculty. Mohler first encouraged her to explore the matter with the trustees of the seminary but, according to Garland, subsequently informed her that there would be no further appeal to the trustees.[18]

Believing she had exhausted all internal remedies and fearing the implications of her resignation for the viability of the Carver School, Dean Garland instead went public with her concerns and criticisms. This action was perceived by the administration as insubordination, for which her appointment as dean was terminated. Garland claims she was fired, while others claim it was a "forced resignation." In any case, both her removal and the new litmus test that had prompted the controversy were endorsed by the trustees a short time later.

When I visited the campus later in 1995 to conduct my interviews, the fate of the Carver School was still undecided. Since that time, Southern Seminary has sold the Carver School to a small undergraduate Baptist college, but the graduate program has closed. Carver students from Southern have transferred to other schools to complete their degrees, and the Southern faculty who resigned (and David Sherwood) worked to establish two new graduate programs. Diana Garland joined an existing social work program at Baylor University with the charge of developing a graduate program to "carry on the legacy of the Carver School." In what she seemed to see as a happy irony—or the completion of a circle—Garland shared that in 2000 she recruited David Sherwood to join the faculty at Baylor.[19]

The Evolution of a Litmus Test

Professor Weber, who was hired in 1992 and who affirmed biblical inerrancy, said that he asked President Mohler if his belief that women may serve as pastors would have precluded his being hired in 1995 and that President Mohler told him that it would have.[20] Inerrancy is no longer the central issue. Southern Seminary has moved from considering a candidate's views on the issue of women's ordination as only an indication of that candidate's views on inerrancy to making hiring decisions solely on the basis of a candidate's views on that issue.

Because women's ordination has always been an issue of contention, one can debate whether this is a new development. But the issue now seems to have taken center stage. Mohler himself previously supported women's ordination.[21] In my interview with him, I asked about his earlier views on women's ordination; he said he had held to the views promoted at the seminary when he was a student there but that as he got out into the larger Baptist community those ideas were challenged and that he had changed his mind through biblical study. David Dockery, vice president for academic affairs and dean of the School of Theology, was scrutinized during a 1992 tenure review before the board for his support of women's ordination;[22] he later grudgingly opposed it, saying that he believed that eventually the members of the denomination would come to support women's ordination but that for the time being he was duty bound to promote the views of those for whom he worked.[23] According to the *Courier Journal*, however, in 1992,

> He did not think the debate [over women's ordination] represented a significant split on the board. He sympathized with trustees who urged a search for teachers who oppose women's ordination. "Different positions on that issue need to be represented."[24]

Clearly, there was always some opposition to the ordination of women as pastors. But early on this was settled by an appeal to Baptist polity; the idea was that Baptists are congregational, with all governing authority remaining with the local church, so if a local congregation wished to call a woman as minister that was the prerogative of that local church. The job of the seminary was simply to train those who wish to seek the call of a local church. While seminary leaders still assert this basic principle, they undermine it at the same time by gradually closing opportunities for such training to women. As many of my respondents at Southern pointed out, it is unlikely that a woman can be well trained for the pastorate when she is trained only by people who do not believe she may hold that position.

The Costs of Purity

Southern Seminary has been willing to pay a very high price to secure agreement on gender-related social issues. While specific reports vary, in 1996, the year following this controversy, the seminary lost approximately one-third of its faculty and one-half of its student body. The Carver School of Social Work was the only school of its kind (i.e., a school of social work attached to a seminary). The air of pain and grief that hung over the campus was as heavy as the summer humidity. Several people spoke of having moved to Louisville in the previous few years to teach at Southern, only to face uprooting their families again because they anticipated leaving or being forced to leave. Others who were older were facing the reality that other schools were unlikely to hire them at this stage in their careers.

People were very careful about their comments for fear of repercussions; during my stay at the school in 1995, several spoke to me only on the condition of anonymity. An atmosphere of intimidation and secrecy pervaded the campus. Diana Garland was, in the end, fired for speaking out about what she believed to be the truth concerning the future of the school of which she was dean. People talked in hushed tones when referring to the controversial issues at hand, even when saying something as seemingly uncontroversial as "Diana Garland is a wonderful person." Appreciation for Garland as a person was apparent in Mohler's own comments and in many of the trustee documents I examined about the incident; yet one person felt the need to whisper the comment when it was made to me in the hallway. A student leader who was sympathetic to Mohler's goals for the seminary and to his views on women told me that he had been given a directive to refrain from talking about "internal matters." Regarding what the students referred to as the "gag rule," a female student said,

> It is very upsetting. Every time that the issue of women in ministry comes up in the classroom, immediately everybody kind of sits on the edge of their chair and it's like ah, well, is the professor going to say something? Is it going to be addressed? Sometimes a professor will just kind of slip over it if it's not really vital to the lesson. If it is a vital part of the lesson, then they will talk about it only as far as it pertains to the subject at hand.

According to student leaders from the Carver School, when they met with Mohler in his office during the peak of the crisis, Mohler's "little assistants" surreptitiously taped the meeting. Students later learned of the taping and requested copies of the tapes, but these were never made available. I was told that there were videotapes of speeches given by Mohler during the Carver School crisis, but when I tried to check them out of the seminary library I was told that they had been "removed from circulation."

Despite my having been immersed in this atmosphere for only a few days, I found myself drawn into the tension, defensiveness, and paranoia. I was in the hallway visiting with an administrator who had talked to me (but only off the record) and who had helped me connect with some other people. We had become friendly and were laughing when President Mohler walked out of an adjacent office. I felt that my being with this person might cause him some difficulty, so I "disappeared," but, since I did so out of reflex, I didn't explain myself at all. Afterward, I laughed to myself when I realized how easy it is to get pulled in when a place has the feel of being "under siege." In my interview with Mohler, I asked him whether he felt embattled, and he replied with a curt "no." His tone was decidedly defensive. I asked him about issues of academic freedom and openness, and he denied that there was an atmosphere in which disagreement was discouraged, let alone squelched. "There are still many on the faculty who disagree with my position on women," he said. When I pointed out that only those with tenure would be free to disagree and that as time went on there would be fewer and fewer of them, he replied, "Yes, but I would want the new conservative faculty members to teach both sides."

Students (both male and female) told me that they regretted having come to Southern. Even one male student who forthrightly proclaimed his support for Mohler's position on women as pastors was clear that he did not support the way in which the changes were being made. A female student told me that she had serious concerns about the quality of education that she, as a woman, would receive and that she was considering changing schools. Her education was being funded by money from the Foreign Missions Board, which told her that her full four years would be covered only if she attends a Southern Baptist school. She believed that the policy changes had not yet trickled down to the classroom and that, as long as there were a few people on faculty who were supportive of her, she could get a good education.

That fundamentalist Southern Baptist leaders would risk destroying their most important seminary over the ordination of women requires explanation. Weber described the turmoil at one meeting with President Mohler:

> I think I've got a pretty tough hide but I think I would have lasted about fifteen minutes in there. . . . People were saying some very raw things about him [Mohler]; accusing him of things, challenging his

competence. . . . And some people said, "But I was, I'm an evangelical and I was hired as an evangelical under a conservative board. But I've had trouble with your view of women and ministry. Does that mean I'm out?" Yeah.

Of the "noncombatants" hired before Sherwood, Weber guessed that, of nineteen people brought in at that time, fourteen were on tenure track or contract and that, of the fourteen, only two or three could pass the new litmus test. He didn't venture a guess about the views of the five who were brought in with tenure. Meanwhile, David Sherwood agreed with the fundamentalists on every point except women's ordination, yet the seminary leaders were intransigent in their opposition to his hiring.

Mohler repeatedly expressed regret over the turmoil caused by these events. But in the end he seemed almost resigned, saying he had done what had to be done and that there had been no other options available to him. His demeanor during my brief interview with him confirmed observations made by others whom I interviewed. While the articulation of a logically consistent ideology may be common, most people find it necessary to have a level of fluidity when they operationalize ideology. For example, it is one thing to make an argument in support of the death penalty; it is another altogether to pull the proverbial switch. Those required to pull the switch commonly exhibit a bit more ambivalence and turmoil. In this case, Mohler did seem completely and consistently governed by his ideology, his theological and philosophical construction for ordering the world. Weber describes a meeting in which "people were weeping"; "they were devastated," scared, and angry. One professor under contract left the room to vomit, and a story circulated (allegedly from an administrator who was there) about Mohler's reaction.[25] According to Weber, he said, "Well that was rough, but I think they understand now." Mohler exhibits a certain emotional detachment from the fallout surrounding his decisions. Weber calls it a "perception problem":

> He doesn't quite—he doesn't read people. He doesn't recognize emotions. The depth of emotions. I think he honestly looks at them as just a disagreement about policy. He's the president, and he and the board have come up with these policies. And his job is to explain it to the faculty and be honest about it, be up front about it, spell it out as plainly as possible. And if he does that that's all he's required to do.

Despite this apparent elevation of reason over emotion, in many ways this conservative transformation of the Southern Baptist denomination was a victory of popular religion over intellectual doctrinal orthodoxy. While both sides grounded their positions in doctrine and biblical exegesis, the power of the more conservative faction seemed more tied to the gut-level reaction evoked by women pastors than to theology. Views on issues like gender have never been considered tests of orthodoxy before, and doctrinal issues over which Christians have died at the hands of other Christians (baptism, the atonement, Calvinism versus Arminianism) are taking a back seat. Regarding a letter about the conflict that appeared in the *Western Recorder* and the power of gender issues to solidify Southern Baptists, Weber said:

> In that letter was the most ingenious, predictable, politically savvy thing you could imagine. In essence, that letter said that what the president is trying to do is hold the line against those evil people who are homosexuals and women as pastors in our churches. You put those two things together and you've got a no-lose approach. You talk about getting rank-and-file Southern Baptists together—you put those two things together. We had no chance. Diana Garland was the enemy . . . she was gone.

The Tables Have Turned

I asked President Mohler how these social issues related to gender had become a litmus test. He told me that it had happened because liberals and conservatives clearly divide on those issues. He explained that those four questions to which candidates must give approved answers are "not the only four issues or even the most important ones; they are just clear dividers in our time. Thirty years from now there will probably be different ones. Thirty years ago no one would have guessed that these would become so important."

In this particular conflict, the southern culture and its gendered dualism may contribute to the clarity of the issues. In most of the conflicts, one side claims gender discrimination, while the other side denies it. While this case is not precisely about gender discrimination, the gender issues are clearly focused, and there is little disagreement over what each side believes. Weber corroborated this, saying,

I don't think there is any other place in the country where there is a longer, stronger entrenched commitment to gender distinctives as there is in the South. You've got the southern-belle syndrome; and that's very much part of this. Women are admired, put on a pedestal, but not taken seriously. Very strong feelings about role differentiation. And so you start messing with this and you are dealing with some very deep kinds of cultural commitments—commitments that evaporated in the North a long time ago with industrialization and all of that.

Fundamentalist leaders believe that, until recently, "liberals" were in control of the institutions of higher education in their denomination. President Mohler asserts that women's ordination is not new as a litmus test; ironically, he believes that support for women's ordination was once an unspoken prerequisite for being hired at Southern, which certainly was the case when I was a student at Fuller. Now the tables are turned, and fundamentalists who control the Southern Baptist Convention and Southern Seminary have placed gender issues at center stage in their battles with moderates in their denomination. The inerrancy of the Bible is no longer the central test of orthodoxy at Southern; it has been replaced by opposition to women's ordination and gay rights.

To this point, we have seen the conflict over women's roles primarily as a battle over ideas and beliefs held and promoted by the central institutions of the conservative Christian world. Having looked at one organization devoted to transforming conservative Christian gender views and at one institution that is fighting such transformation, we now move to explore the impact of these conflicts on the lives of individual women.

* 3 *

Conflict in the
Lives of Individual Women

I had these messages coming at me that I had been carefully nurtured and had been groomed, I had been taken up from the ranks to
be put on the faculty, you know, to show the world that [we] do not
discriminate against women. "Look what we're doing! We have
grown our own here. We're pulling her through. We're going to help
her out through her graduate degree." But what it was [was] just a
little leaf on a tree that's never going to change the full view of the
school which says: Women are not important to God. . . . They keep
saying that "of course you are valuable, *but* . . . "; there's always a *but*
on the end of it. Of course women are equal to men, *but* . . . ;
women can do this in the church, *but* . . . ; women can contribute
this, *but*. . . . And it was playing itself out in my personal life because
if I ever expressed myself to my husband, his immediate response
was to get angry with me and tell me "you can't think those
thoughts, those are wrong."

I argued in the Introduction that it is inadequate to try to understand religion as merely a belief system. Conservative Christians disagree on many
beliefs, ranging from ideas about the proper mode of baptism to views on
the end times. Not all even claim to be biblical literalists. What they do
share, however, is a cultural identity, and if this is the case, it pushes us to
explore these conflicts over gender as more than institutional battles for
power. The struggle for power within the conservative Protestant movement creates tremendous turmoil and conflict in the day-to-day lives of
individual members of the community. Because the idea of having
women serve in leadership positions as pastors and in important roles in

conservative Christian colleges and seminaries is so contested, issues naturally arise when they do serve in these roles; because there is not a clear separation among work, family, and faith in these women's lives, the conflict often has an impact on all three. This makes the lives of women in these positions a natural arena in which to explore the way these conflicts play out in the lives of real people. This chapter is built around the stories of women who are continuously called on to justify their positions of leadership and the situations they face: what they call their "war stories." I draw on formal interviews with women in pastoral roles in churches and in parachurch ministries, as well as the stories of women in elite positions at evangelical educational institutions. My discussion is based on the stories as told by the women themselves. Because of the sensitivity of these cases, I have changed the names of people and institutions to protect their anonymity. While I have corroborated these stories sufficiently to know that they are not fabrications, I have not attempted to determine whether gender discrimination has "actually" occurred, and I recognize that the institutions and many of the people involved may view these cases differently. I present these women's stories as examples of the kinds of issues these women believe they face and to illuminate the ways in which they respond to what they see as tension-filled situations. The recurrence of similar problems and accusations in churches and schools across the country lends credibility to the broader themes, even if the interpretation of any individual story can be disputed.

Women as Pastors

Evangelical seminaries report increasing enrollment of women in degree programs leading to pastoral ministry. Two decades ago, James Davison Hunter found widespread commitment to women's equality among future evangelical leaders (who, by now, should have assumed those leadership roles).[1] But what happens to the seminary-educated women when they complete their training and seek pastoral positions? What special difficulties do they face? How are they received by the members of their congregations? By their colleagues?

Many seminary-trained women end up not actually becoming pastors but using their training in other ways. In an interview with the (male) assistant pastor at a very large church, which is the one of the better-known churches in a denomination founded by a woman, I questioned why, given the history of the denomination, there were not more women serving as senior pastors. The pastor agreed that there were few women serving as pastors in his denomination and explained this by saying that it seemed to be a response to the market. "Most people don't want a woman as senior pastor. Women who do pastor churches rarely build them up to be large churches; they tend to stay small." One woman pastor explained that women have a tougher time and are more closely scrutinized than men:

> I know several women who graduated from seminary with high hopes but have not found appropriate placement. There was always something—related to marital situation, grades, age, personality, theological background, whatever—that caused the potential lead to disappear.
>
> In our denomination, most churches are too small for more than one pastor on staff. That makes a problem, because many women *want* associate positions, and some superintendents don't think of women as good "preaching pastor" candidates even though our denomination *says* we're in favor of it. So there aren't that many appropriate openings.

When women find positions in evangelical churches, it is increasingly common for those positions to be as part of a "pastoral team," often as husband and wife. These are rarely situations in which there is parity in the status accorded to both team members, in their functions, or in their salaries. Lisa R. Avalos-Bock finds examples in the Vineyard church she studied in which women appear to have equal access to leadership but are, in fact, limited to a subordinate role.

> Vineyard church planting teams are typically structured around a married couple who will "pastor" the new church according to gendered role expectations. Among these couples the man functions as the actual pastor while the woman performs an adjunct, supportive role. Thus, although Vineyard pastors and their wives are typically referred to as "pastoral couples," the terminology deceptively suggests that women function as pastors when in fact they do not. The roles of house group pastor and church planter rely on married couples for their fulfillment and they channel women into puppet roles that are devoid of real decision making power or institutional respect.[2]

In examples from my own fieldwork, one church had a husband and wife on the pastoral staff. The husband called himself the senior pastor; the wife called herself and her husband a pastoral team. He was paid more money, had his office in the main church building, preached all the Sunday services and most of the midweek services, and ran all the business meetings. The female co-pastor had her office in the "Sunday school building," which was a house next door. She was responsible for the women's discipleship groups, the Sunday school program, and the production of the church bulletin. Among church members, she was referred to as "a pastor," but the husband was called "*the* pastor."

Even a woman pastor I spoke with who asserted that her husband "fully share[d her] view of biblical equality" and that she and her husband shared "the position of pastor/founder [of their church] on an equal basis" reported a significant disparity in the roles they performed. "His main responsibility [was] to lead and preach the Sunday morning services," which she "help[ed] lead." She preached about once per month. They both took "an active part in all the leadership training and program planning." She was responsible for all the clerical work, the music, and the children's ministry, while his unique responsibilities were to lead the Wednesday night Bible study, to counsel people, to study, and to pray. He also "help[ed] with the children's church" and was "helping" the youth leader get started.

In another example, a woman named Paula worked as a youth pastor on the staff of a well-known parachurch ministry. She told me of her experiences at a summer camp where she was supposed to be "coworker boss."[3]

> "Co" means I am the female—and what I faced . . . I had never experienced [in another context]. He entirely sabotaged any leadership for me for the entire month that I was there. He obviously didn't believe in women leadership. His marriage was extremely traditional, his wife was always at home with the kids—she had her little role of helping and he was in charge and so he treated me that way.

When I asked her for specific examples of how her male coworker did this, she told me,

> We were together supposed to make all of the decisions for the camp and it was expected that way. He would just go alone to all the camp directors

and supervisors and make all these decisions and then he would come out and tell everybody about them without even telling me—and I would go out to make an announcement to the kids and he would cut me off or correct me or challenge what I was saying. He wanted to be in charge. That was clear.

But Paula recognized that if she were to make an issue of his behavior, she would appear petty and "un-Christian." The points of conflict were subtle enough, and taken for granted enough, that most people wouldn't have even noticed them. Paula, like many women in similar situations, even struggled within herself, questioning whether her discomfort with the situation was a result of her own sinfulness.

> It was this conservative evangelical spiritual guilt I was living with. If we weren't getting along I mustn't be being a good enough Christian. I just needed to pray, or I needed to pray for forgiveness. . . . I didn't know that male-female dynamic could go on because I had never experienced it before.

Unlike women who work on pastoral teams with their husbands, Paula did have some ability to address the inequity she perceived by raising the issue with her superiors. But when she went to talk to her supervisor about the problem, the supervisor carried on about what a wonderful Christian man her coworker was and, blind to the gender-related problems she was experiencing, how wonderful he was to work with. "I felt crazy. What is wrong with me that I can't work with this wonderful Christian man who everyone thinks is so wonderful?"

The prevalence of self-doubt like that expressed by Paula is remarkable; I found it in nearly all of the conflicts I examined. It is exacerbated by the subtle but broad-based undermining of women's self-confidence. Women's essential nature is thought to be dependent, designed for supportive rather than leadership roles, and in need of masculine leadership and guidance. With such socialization, women, more than men, look to others to validate their interpretations of situations and their own understandings of their talents and callings.

> In Bible school my husband and I were engaged. During that time we would often talk with students and leaders and it always hurt me when they asked him what he thought God had called him to do, but they never

asked me, even though I was standing right there beside him and they knew I had sacrificed a lot to leave my country and family to pursue the ministry.

Another woman who did become a pastor told me,

> I just remember lots of comments to the effect that, "Well if you're going to be a minister, well certainly you'll marry a pastor and be a pastor's wife. And that would be a way you could minister." Well, I didn't marry a pastor. I didn't find any I wanted to marry and that was never my intent anyway.

It was not uncommon for women to report direct, public challenges to their serving in pastoral roles. One pastor, whom I'll call Mary, was serving as an assistant pastor, and her senior pastor was to be out of town on a communion Sunday. A man in the church who opposed Mary's ministry threatened to walk out if she served communion. In the end, his effort failed, but she recalled the fear with which she had approached the pulpit the first time she was to preach. In addition to the common anxiety about speaking in front of a group that most new pastors face, Mary was aware that many in her congregation thought that "the church roof would fall in if a woman preached." The church even set up a special microphone from which she was to address the congregation. The microphone was in the front of the sanctuary but not on the platform from which the men spoke.

Cindy reported that when she and her husband were working as traveling ministers, taking turns preaching, she had several such experiences. "I've had people leave the meeting when it was my turn to preach, explaining later that the Bible didn't allow them to 'submit to a woman.'" Women also reported being hired as pastors only to find that the job requirements changed once they were there. Having been emphatic during the hiring process that she was interested only in a pastoral position (she was applying to be an assistant pastor), Mary arrived on her first Sunday to find that the church bulletin had introduced her as the "new staff person in the office."

> They did attempt, right at first, to turn me into a children's pastor regardless of the titles I had or the job I had been hired to do. . . . One woman

took me out to lunch, you know, really gave me a talking to about it. Because that was "what I really should be doing there."

Many career women report facing assumptions and pressures to conform to gendered expectations at work. In these cases those assumptions and pressures take on added significance because of the intimacy of the relationship between congregation members and their spiritual leaders.

But there are structural limitations on women's roles as well. Paula, my respondent from the parachurch ministry, explained that men who were important leaders in her organization were made "area leaders" (AL) while women were typically made "staff women." It was the "area leaders" who were considered the "real leadership." Even when the position of area leader was opened to women and Paula became one, she was still sidelined in terms of authority. Men whom she was supposed to oversee in her area resented having a woman in authority over them. While the institution had reached the point where it wanted to promote women and give them equality, its leadership tried to achieve this in a way that would be palatable to those who disagreed with the policy.

> My biggest pain in the organization was how frustrating it was that it actually had a mission purpose statement that said that women should be in leadership but they wouldn't hold their staff accountable. They wouldn't—I would say they didn't have the courage, and they didn't want to lose people.

The organization recruited women as workers, encouraged them to seek promotion to positions of increasing leadership responsibility, and then put them in difficult positions by not supporting their efforts. The organizations were trying to transform the roles of women and at the same time placate those who opposed having women in leadership positions, the organization failed to require its members to accept Paula and other women in the leadership roles they had been given.

A woman who worked as both a pastor and an administrator at a nearby seminary experienced similar difficulties when she occupied a leadership role but lacked institutional support.

> It is much harder to function in my seminary position as a woman. Yikes! The structure is very hierarchical. . . . I am often ignored (the greatest

insult) or simply not consulted in matters, even for which I have shouldered the greatest responsibility! I am weary right now with being a woman in this man's world of the seminary. I am more horrified at the lack of integration with my male colleagues' and superiors' Christianity and their "business" than I am with the church.

Another woman was invited to give several talks at a camp meeting that was attended by boys, girls, and their youth leaders. When she got up to speak, a couple of the male youth leaders folded their arms and turned their backs on her.

> You learn in the leadership manual that the leaders are supposed to be looking attentively at the speaker and really into it, and trying to get their kids into it, and there were several men who modeled disrespect toward me, who would not bring their kids up to meet me, acted like I didn't exist.

This same woman told me how another youth leader came up to her and in what she perceived as a ridiculing tone asked her how it felt to be "breaking the ice." She told me that when she noted that she was not the first woman camp speaker, the male youth leader responded,

> Yeah and people really didn't like her much because of it either, did they? All I can say is any woman who I ever see stick around [in leadership] for a while gets really manly, becomes really manly and unfeminine.

Another common problem faced by women who, in a strongly gendered subculture, move into positions that have traditionally been reserved for men is that they simply do not fit in in many job-related social situations. Pamela, a woman who pastored a small church, told me that she ran into very few conflicts in her own congregation, since people would be unlikely to become members if they weren't comfortable with her leadership. Significant conflicts arose, however, as a result of her participation in denominational meetings and retreats. She told me of a pastor's meeting, for example, in which the program indicated that there would be separate meetings for men and women.

> I had no indication of what the meeting was about or anything. I had no opportunity to talk to the leader or anything to find out if it was some kind of meeting or a social time or what—it turns out that it [the men's

meeting] was for pastors in which there was a great deal of information distributed. It was actually a professional meeting.

Pamela learned about the men's meeting from the wife of another pastor who had attended with her husband. But, as Pamela said, if she had made an issue of the lack of clarity over who was invited to attend, someone would have said, "So what's the big deal? Why are you making a big deal about it?" They might have even dismissed her concerns by calling her "a woman's libber," a term some employ within conservative Christianity to indicate that someone is not to be taken seriously. While it is common for wives to attend conferences and retreats with their pastor husbands, when Pamela's husband joined her at the meetings he was often teased and made to feel uncomfortable. Often, though, the others in attendance assumed that he was the pastor and that she was there with him.

Women who reported receiving tremendous support from the members of their congregations often found that disheartening roadblocks were put in place by other religious leaders who withheld the cooperation that would normally be accorded a male colleague. Victoria, who has pastored a nondenominational church for six years, reported that the lack of support from other pastors in her community made it more difficult for her to perform her ministry responsibilities. A woman in her church approached Victoria with a desire to be baptized by immersion. Victoria's church did not have a baptistery, so she contacted a church she had previously attended for sixteen years and requested permission to use theirs. The request was approved, and the baptism took place. Later, Victoria asked to use the baptistery a second time, and her friend at the church explained that he had not previously informed the board that she would actually be doing the baptism. Once the board learned this, it refused permission for her to use its facility.

Another pastor faced a similar situation when she was asked to lead a retreat for a group of churches. "When the retreat center [at which the retreat was to be held] learned that a woman was to be the main speaker, they did not allow us to come."

Each of these situations served to remind the women pastors that they were not fully accepted in their leadership roles. In several instances, reactions from congregation members or colleagues limited their ability to function properly in these roles. As we shall see, other leadership positions involve similar difficulties and conflicts.

Women in the Christian Academy

Evangelicals who work to educate young Christians in evangelical colleges and seminaries have special authority; they are responsible for maintaining and transmitting the "faith once delivered to the saints" and are charged with the reproduction of the religious culture and its transmission to the next generation.

Parents send their children to these colleges for the express purpose of shoring up their children's faith at a time when many other young people experience profound intellectual and spiritual challenges. People called to "serve the Lord" in these roles see their work as just that: a calling. Within the American Protestant movement they are often accorded the esteem that pastors and teachers in the larger culture lost quite some time ago.

The emphasis on the timeless truths of the Gospel and on the popular notion that the Christian tradition is unchanging creates a worldview in which it is difficult to account for variations in Christian teachings. All of the schools represented here at some level endorse the participation of women as leaders and teachers. But that support is not monolithic within these institutions, and, as with the debate over whether women should serve as pastors, these discrepancies create tension, turmoil, and conflict. Women who serve in Christian higher education constantly face critics who argue with them about the legitimacy of their functioning in those roles and sometimes subtly undermine their positions. Many of these conflicts have culminated in problematic tenure reviews and the firing of the women involved.

If these academic institutions are important sites of cultural production—and if the roles of women are points of conflict in the subculture—then the position of women in important roles in these institutions should be extremely problematic. It is. My interviews with nineteen women in important positions at Christian colleges and seminaries, as well as my interviews with three men who have served as mentors to such women and with several students who have had these women as professors, bore this out.[4]

All of my respondents indicated that the number of women in full-time tenured or tenure-track academic posts in conservative Christian institutions is quite small.

> When we go to faculty meetings its very deceiving because it looks as if we have about a forty/sixty ratio. . . . When you walk in you see a lot of

women. But you sit down and you start counting the full-time teaching faculty who are on tenure track, the number who are women—the number gets very small.

In addition to part-time and nontenure-track teaching positions, which are often held by women, positions such as librarian and counselor (which are also often held by women) are also often counted as faculty posts. One professor at another evangelical college told me that her institution boasted that it had hired many women, but the numbers were deceiving:

> Often on campus here they say, "Oh, we're doing better in terms of hiring women because there are more women on the faculty." And that is true; there are more women on the faculty. But almost all of them are in education and a higher percent of them don't have Ph.D.s. . . . The other thing they point to [is that] we've just hired a woman dean. Well, we have, but before we hired her we demoted her position. The dean of faculty used to report directly to the president. Now the dean of faculty reports to the provost who reports to the president. So we demoted her position and then we were willing to hire a woman.

Many women in my research claimed that they had faced discrimination in hiring, but, because of the confidentiality of the hiring process, they rarely had much more than their suspicion to go on. One of the most persistent problems in examining the issues in these cases was that it is often impossible to consider all the relevant perspectives because confidentiality requirements rendered many of the facts inaccessible. It was not uncommon for women to tell me that they themselves had not been given explanations for decisions that had been made regarding their jobs. Helen's school was experiencing some confusion about the "nature and function" of the role of the board of trustees in the hiring process, which affected her job. A woman in her fifties, Helen had a Ph.D. in her field and many years' teaching experience, and she had even served as the department chair at her previous institution. Having married a tenured professor, she sought to relocate so that the couple could be together. She was interviewed and hired by the administration at the college where her husband teaches. Her hiring was conditioned on the approval of the board of trustees, which did not meet until after she had relocated and begun teaching.

Before being interviewed by the trustees, Helen spoke with another woman who had appeared before them during her application process and had been "grilled" on the legitimacy of having a Christian woman teach men in light of Paul's edicts against allowing women to have authority over men. It was Helen's view that the gendered attack had been so blatant that the board ultimately decided that it would be putting itself at risk for legal action if it opted not to hire the applicant, and so it did hire her. Helen concluded, however, that the board also decided to be more careful in the future. Helen described her interview with the board as very brief and emphasized that she went into the meeting determined to come across as a "nice person who didn't want to make waves." She now believes that the interview was a farce.

> Well, in retrospect I'm sure that the ducks were gotten in order and when they interviewed me in the fall, it was a foregone conclusion that I would not be allowed to teach. They handled it rather well in terms of any repercussions from it because they gave me no reasons. They just kept me there for a few minutes and pretty much dismissed me and told me I couldn't teach.

But, according to Helen, the board did indicate that she could teach if her husband were to supervise her classes. She decided to teach at another Christian college, and she and her husband had to live apart temporarily.

Helen experienced extra tension created by the fact that the school was speaking with multiple voices regarding the roles of women. In her case, the board of trustees (which ultimately had the power to make hiring decisions) opposed having women in certain roles in the Christian community, while the faculty and the administration wanted to bring about change.

> You get women caught in the middle like me who bear the pain. . . . The faculty couldn't say anything. They didn't really understand—so much cognitive dissonance. The president and the dean didn't dare say anything, so who's left? And I thought it was interesting that evidently in their five-year plan—one faculty woman raised the question, "There is nothing in here about having women on faculty." And the president said, "I got burned on that one." Which I'm sure means with hiring me and being told he couldn't keep me. . . . So they are not really able to be honest. Officially, their position is that women shouldn't be ordained. But

then you have all this fallout, too, they can't see them in other leadership positions.

Women seeking posts that do not involve teaching encountered difficulties in the hiring process based on age-old arguments about the complications that arise when men and women work together. An administrator at a meeting of Christian College Coalition Presidents asked why there were not more high-level female administrators. She reported that sixteen of the twenty-three said they couldn't have a woman in a position that required travel because they "couldn't travel with a woman because of the appearance of evil."

All of the female professors I interviewed were considered by their students to be excellent teachers.[5] One woman told me of a conversation she had had with the president of her college:

> He said to me, "Joanne, we were astounded when you came because enrollment in our sociology classes just swelled. In fact, we had to close classes and there were still students wanting to take the courses."

Another woman who was eventually let go after being embroiled in a difficult tenure review showed me the stack of letters and cards her students had sent to encourage her. They had organized a petition drive, written editorials in the school paper, and demanded meetings with the president in which they asked him to explain the decision to fire her. Student after student wrote that she was the best teacher he or she had had, that her courses had changed students' lives, and that the school would not be the same without her. While the case was discussed in the school paper for months—and many students wrote of their support for her—I did not find even one article that was critical of her classroom performance. The tenure review committee conducted interviews with students in order to evaluate her performance and found widespread support. Students were asked, as part of their class evaluations, about her teaching abilities and consistently indicated that she was an excellent teacher. The review also indicated that the space provided to list "weaknesses" was most often empty. The teacher indicated to me that she had received some of the highest scores accorded anyone at this stage of the tenure process.

Across the board, female students indicated that they see having female faculty as role models and mentors as extremely important to their education. Support for female teachers was not unanimous, however; most of the women teachers I interviewed said that they had always had a few students who were opposed to women teaching in higher education and that they had been challenged in the classroom. One professor told me that she had been told by students that there was a lot of "negative talk around campus [about her being] a 'feminist' and that [she] should just be avoided."

> Some guys said that women shouldn't teach theology, and a guy walked in one day and wanted to know where my hat was [a reference to Paul's admonition that women should have their heads covered when "praying or prophesying in church"]. A lot of guys just avoided my classes. They would say, "Who would want to take a theology course taught by a woman, anyway?"

Several female professors told me that they had encountered subtle disrespect from students who called them by their first names but who addressed men professors by their surnames. Other students insisted on calling them "Mrs." instead of "Dr." Joanne told me of a female colleague who was an accomplished professor but whom students insisted on treating as if she were one of them.

> They actually had coordinated efforts to disrupt her classroom, to disrupt her teaching. And there were rumors going around that she was "an old maid." I mean, this woman is thirty-six years old, married, and has three kids. I really think it was because she was a woman and she doesn't wear a wedding band. They couldn't quite place her in an appropriate role and they didn't want to learn from her. . . . I just find it so intriguing that because the students couldn't place her, they didn't respect her.

Eventually the department intervened and informed the students of the professor's qualifications, publication record, and marital status, and, according to Joanne, in the next semester she was able to "reassert" herself.

The most blatant example of students' challenging the legitimacy of a woman, according to Joanne, was the story of what happened in her sociology course in gender relations. The first time the course was taught, forty-five students signed up, including, Joanne told me, two who had been told by their advisers that they should take the course but who came in bent on being disruptive. On a campus where jeans and tee-shirts were typical student attire, these two young men came to the first day of class in "dark suits, ties, and polished shoes." They sat together in the front row with computers on their desks. "This was power. This was real symbolic power," she said.

> They interrupted me every other sentence. I could not get through my material. They were extremely rude. One of them would write a word down [on the computer] and say, "you just used this word, now can you please define for me what you mean by this word?" Just being extremely disrespectful and disruptive. Purposely trying to take control of the class-room, making a big joke out of it.

This continued outside the classroom, as well. One of the same young men came to Joanne's office with the books that had been assigned for the class.

> He threw them down on the floor and said they were trash. That he had worked in Washington, D.C., and he was really sick of women like me and people who were trying to teach the ideas that I was trying to teach. . . . And he started saying, "Have you read these books?" Here I am, I am the one with the Ph.D., and he's asking me if I've read the books! And he had just already typed me as a certain type of person. . . . He had not even heard my ideas yet. He hadn't taken the course. He hadn't read the books. He had just already decided where I fit into all this and that I didn't be-long there.

Women also reported being challenged as to why they were not home with their children. A female seminary professor told me about going into the school bookstore to order a book on women and power in nonprofit organizations that was not available in her library. A student clerk in the bookstore proceeded to give her a thirty-minute "lecture" as to why she "should not be reading books like that because it would simply make [her] angry and that wasn't doing [her] any good and that, after all, a woman's highest calling is to be a wife and mother."

That students feel free to challenge faculty members in the manner il-lustrated by these examples points to the effectiveness of the strategies used to reproduce gender norms and expectations. Students, by virtue of the way women are treated in this subculture, come to see such responses as appropriate and acceptable.

When Carol was finishing her Ph.D., she was hired by her seminary to teach a homiletics course. She was congratulated by a male fellow student who said, "Oh, are you going to teach a woman's section?" She replied, "As a matter of fact, this section is all men." She told me that "the look on his face was just one of absolute horror. I mean he literally backed away from me physically because I was going to be teaching men in this homiletics class."

Many women who work as the only woman in a department or as one of only a few on their faculty find that they have to take on the extra task of "representing" women. They end up serving on more committees than their male counterparts and mentoring more students than their male colleagues. One woman who was asked to speak for the "women on the campus" in an accreditation evaluation refused to do so.

> I am one woman on this campus, and I can't speak for every woman on the campus. My feeling was that they should speak to a number of women and get a number of viewpoints. And, also, I'm just real tired of being the person who is supposed to be the spokesperson for women's issues when I was hired to be a sociologist. I'm getting pulled too far from my teaching. And I also think it lets the college off the hook.

Many women in my study found themselves embroiled in controversy when they raised the issue of using gender-inclusive language. Carol read an article on salvation in which a former member of the faculty on which she served had used masculine pronouns throughout. She wrote him what she said was a "nice" letter telling him she greatly enjoyed the article but suggesting that his choice of gender-exclusive language made salvation seem available only to men. The author of the article responded by accusing her of "worshipping mother-God and being a secular feminist and leaving [her] biblical roots." He sent a copy of his letter to the president of Carol's institution and said that he was "appalled" that someone with her views could be on their faculty.

The most visible point at which these women confronted gender-related problems, though, was during their tenure reviews. A study of the faculty at Seattle Pacific University found that

> 76% of the men were promoted the first time they requested it and 76% of the women were denied promotion the first time they requested it. The reasons for denial according to the women varied from "in-house" deci-

sions in their departments to being told that they were "not ready" with little elaboration. Other denials were made at the academic administrative level with reasons for denial such as "not collegial" or "not enough service to the university" or "questionable Christian commitment.[6]

The women I interviewed reported that the problems they faced most often centered on their working relationships with their male colleagues. Because most faculties have a very limited number of women, it is common for there to be no women, or at most only one woman, on the tenure review committee. This leaves the schools open to charges of sexism in their tenure decisions whether or not sexism could ever be proved.

In one case, the woman who was up for tenure review was evaluated on eight points that were considered essential elements for success as a Christian scholar. Most elements had objective criteria, and a few had relatively objective measurements. For example, student evaluations and enrollment in courses were used to evaluate teaching performance, and publication records and listings of honors received were used to evaluate professional development. This particular candidate scored very highly on seven categories but failed two of five subpoints of the last category. These subpoints had to do solely with judgments made by other members of her department, several of whom criticized her for lack of "collegiality."

In these controversial tenure review cases, in which the woman under review feels that many of the problems she faces stem from gender-related differences, lack of collegiality is the most common criticism. Many of the women believed that this problem arises from essential differences in the ways men and women relate to each other. In fact, at least one woman believed that this is a no-win situation for women because the behaviors that men use to demonstrate collegiality are understood differently when women use them. She argued that men can demonstrate a professional deference to a more senior colleague, but if a female colleague behaves in the same way it is interpreted as a gendered deference rather than a professional one. For example, in a debate over an issue in a faculty meeting, a junior faculty member might defer the floor to a more senior faculty member as a matter of professional deference. But if a woman makes the same move, her action might be perceived as gendered deference. Furthermore, should a woman fail to make such a move, she would be seen as violating both professional and gender etiquette. The particular scholar I interviewed is both a respected scholar on gender issues and the survivor of a gender-related conflict in a hiring dispute. She contended, on the basis of both her experience and scholarship, that there are no ways for women to show purely professional deference.

While "collegiality" might seem innocuous as an evaluation criterion, its potential for misuse arising from its vague and subjective character has been widely recognized and debated. In 1999, the American Association of University Professors stated its support for the traditional evaluation criteria of teaching, scholarship, and service and its opposition to the addition of a fourth category: collegiality. AAUP's argument was that collegiality was implicit in the traditional three categories and that making it a fourth independent category threatened diversity, academic freedom, and legitimate dissent.[7]

Women are also often accused of being "controlling" and "aggressive" and speculate that men who behave as they do would not be so labeled. And yet more "feminine" teaching styles that are nondirective and that emphasize creative teaching are not respected. Women in Christian settings are also often criticized as "self-promoting." Ambition is not considered appropriate to Christian character, especially to feminine Christian character. Humility and selflessness are praised. But when institutions are structured in such a way as to encourage and promote men into increasingly responsible positions while leaving women to succeed on their own, women believe they have little alternative but to make known their own achievements. Several women I interviewed relayed stories about the moments they first realized that they could not rely on their male superiors to be their advocates. Rachel, a high-level administrator, had been encouraged by her boss and mentor to apply for promotion to a position about which he would make the hiring decision.

> So I just sort of naively assumed that this man for whom I had worked for six years . . . would be my advocate in this whole process. . . . I thought, you know, "All this hard work has really paid off. He has noticed what a good job I've done and I got my doctorate, and you know, all this."

According to Rachel, the job went to a "big-talking" man with a B.A. and only five years' experience. He was perceived as more qualified than Rachel, who had a Ph.D. and twelve years' experience. What was most devastating to Rachel was that, while her mentor told her that the committee had wanted to hire the man, she later learned from individual committee members that the committee had actually voted to give the job to her; the decision to hire Rachel's male competitor had been made by the man she thought had been her mentor.

Additional tension is created within many parts of the evangelical sub-culture because it is seen as a moral duty to pass judgment on, and comment on, what would be considered personal issues in most other circles.

In one example of this, Rachel had been hired as a high-level administrator for a Christian college. She moved to the town in which the college was located, but her husband stayed behind for a year because they had a son in his senior year of high school. During Rachel's first year at her new job, the family decided that it didn't want to move. Rachel's new college was too isolated, rural, and remote, and her husband would have had to move from a tenured position to an untenured one and take a significant pay cut. Any couple facing such a decision would have found it difficult, but Rachel's situation was further complicated by the fact that the school that employed her saw itself as having a role to play in the decision. She explained:

> Well, [our decision not to move our family] sent everyone into a royal tizzy. The board of trustees had to talk about it in executive session and they were speculating on our marriage and what kind of husband did I have who is allowing me to do this—it was really something—they said something about our sex life and speculated on whether we were going to get a divorce. They said I wasn't a good role model for the women students.

Rachel had been promised a three-year contract at the end of her first year. When she was given another one-year contract, she was told that the reason was that her husband had not moved to join her. Moreover, the board did not make it at all clear how it would evaluate her success in the course of that year.

The women interviewed often complained that they perceived a lack of specificity regarding the evaluation criteria. Many expressed a feeling that they were on trial without knowing the charges. They often acknowledged that this impression put them on the defensive, giving credibility to some of the criticisms others leveled at them.

> There must be some other criteria that I'm going to be measured on, and I don't know what [they are]. And that's very worrisome to me . . . I read

things into everything people say and I just become very paranoid. I find myself not being very courageous or adventuresome as I would have been. I feel like I'm always looking over my shoulder because I don't know who is talking about me behind my back. And trying to hear what they are saying so I know what is really going on.

To summarize, family requirements that go along with being a "good evangelical" in the context of gendered expectations about work often create no-win situations for these professional women. In the study of Seattle Pacific University, 86 percent of the women experienced family-related interruptions in their graduate study. Because of family responsibilities, the women also took, on average, two years longer to achieve their promotions than men.[8]

Rachel's job was in jeopardy because she and her husband were employed at different schools (her husband faced no such issues in his position); like so many couples employed in higher education, they had to endure a long-distance relationship. On the other hand, in another case, a woman reported being repeatedly belittled by colleagues who asserted that, her good qualifications aside, she was hired as part of a "package deal" with her husband. Being married and having children is also essential to being seen as a full-fledged adult member of the community. One female professor said:

One thing I have really struggled with here is that there was, maybe, even "relief" in my having kids—I've had people on campus talk to me for the first time when I got married. . . . I think they put you in a different category or something.

She went on to say that women who were not married or who did not have children were viewed as younger than other women and therefore were not taken as seriously and had less power. She added that men were not evaluated in the same way. While it is obviously not a written part of the criteria for evaluation, having a family is a factor in the general perception about the kind of person the woman faculty member is. A "double-bind" is created: despite the community requirement that a good evangelical will have a family, family responsibilities are assumed to fall primarily on women and none of the time she spends performing them counts when her job performance is being evaluated.

The young women studying in conservative Christian colleges and seminaries are preparing to take the places of the leaders from whom we have already heard. Life in a Christian college is, in some sense, the culmination of the process of introducing a young evangelical to the life of an adult member of the community. The ways in which gender issues are treated in this context are reflective of cultural perspectives about gender and, at the same time, productive of gender norms, expectations, and beliefs for the future.

This chapter is drawn from research at seven schools in different parts of the country between 1993 and 1995, including nine formal interviews of male and female students and many more informal conversations. I attended a conference designed to foster mentoring relationships between women Christian college faculty and students, a semester-long feminist theology tutorial, and several on-campus lectures, and I conducted brief random surveys on the campuses of three of the colleges. I have also drawn from a collection of letters, clippings, and personal statements from Christian college students pertaining to specific events related to gender issues.[9]

Girls typically outnumber boys at evangelical colleges. Many Christian parents send their sons to secular colleges and universities but insist that their daughters go to Christian colleges in hopes of keeping them protected from "the world." A member of the admissions committee at one evangelical college told me that the school had an affirmative action program for boys; boys with lower test scores and grades were admitted over some girls with higher marks in an effort to have some balance in the number of boys and girls.[10] One pastor who was the father of both a girl and a boy told me he wanted his son to go the relatively prestigious UCLA because that would better his career prospects but that he wanted his daughter to go to the conservative Bible Institute of Los Angeles (BIOLA) because it was near their home and offered a "safe" environment. The underlying assumption (in addition to his "safety" concern) was that a career was less likely to be important to his daughter's future than to his son's.

More than a few students told me that it was still common at these schools for girls to admit that they came to college to find a husband.

I've been here for four years and the prevailing attitudes I've encountered—from males and females—I feel have been really sexist and narrow-minded. I mean, I just remember the first week of school sitting in the dining hall, a bunch of girls telling me, the reason they are here is just they want to find a husband.

Each spring, in what seems reminiscent of a 1950s movie about college coeds, "senior panic" overtakes the young women who are about to graduate and are not yet engaged to be married. And those young women who come to college with goals for the future find that, at many points, they are steered away from career goals and encouraged to focus on marriage and family. They feel this pressure not only from their institutions but also from their peers. There is pervasive hostility to feminism, and very few students were willing to identify themselves by that label.[11] Contrary to evidence found by Hunter two decades ago,[12] very few students in my surveys were aware of the evangelical feminist movement or had heard of the major evangelical feminist groups. Female faculty members with whom I talked, who had attended Christian colleges themselves, indicated that they believed that attitudes about women's issues had grown increasingly polarized over the years since they were undergraduates.

At one college, a group of young women went to considerable effort to organize a feminist theology tutorial to be led by a female member of the religious studies department, and even some of these young women were reluctant to call themselves feminists. During the course of the semester, each came to a point where she embraced the label "feminist," and a couple of them reported this transition as a real breakthrough for them. These same women reported being criticized by fellow students for being seen reading books about women. One young man saw one of these women in the student lunchroom reading a book with the word "women" in the title and launched into an extended lecture about how she shouldn't be reading such things. This tutorial had been offered more than once over the course of a few years, and several of the women who took it reported that they felt hostility, not only from students but also from faculty members in their religious studies department. "I began to sense a new attitude toward me in the RS department. . . . I felt all but a few of the RS professors cool toward me." Another young woman said,

> There was a definite shift in attitudes from the religious studies department after I began the tutorial. It is difficult to explain. There was almost a stiffening towards me, an avoidance of the topic of "the feminist theology class." However, it became increasingly clear that many of my peers and professors were wary of my involvement in this class.

On one campus, there was a group of students, both male and female; who met regularly with a male professor for intellectual and spiritual discipleship. When several women in this tight-knit group began asking questions about the treatment of women in the history of their tradition and started reading feminist books, they were ostracized from the group and ridiculed by fellow students.

> This was such an awkward time. I was full of questions and the desire to search for a deeper understanding of my spirituality, my role as a woman, my God. I needed to ask questions such as, "Why is God father and not mother?" The mere question has turned into deviant behavior at this point as I was labeled "the feminist." I had friends tell me that people I did not even know on campus thought I was opinionated and abrasive. I had no idea that a few women studying one topic and asking honest questions could stir so much emotion. I felt bullied by people I did not know well as they joked about the "femi-nazi" and "apostate."

At one point, these young women were called before a special meeting of the discipleship group (the meeting was called by the faculty member who led the group) to "address the discomfort felt by other members as a result of the tutorial." This young women reports that she was

> accused of "changing" and "being angry and hostile." [We were] all attacked and unjustly accused. I certainly had misgivings about their perception of my attitude and behavior, but I was even more shocked by what the group said about the other women in my tutorial. By the end of the meeting we were all in tears. While I cannot fully understand or explain my professor's role in this antagonism, I do believe that both he and our peers were extremely uncomfortable that we might be feminists.

Women at every school I visited reported feeling steered away from careers toward marriage and family as their only occupation. The pressure they perceived was sometimes blatant and intentional, sometimes more subtle and resulted from pervasive attitudes about women and their appropriate roles. I obtained a list of women alumnae from one school and counted 167 graduates with religious studies majors. While the expectation that religious studies would be good preparation for seminary is reasonable, only 13 of the 167 graduates reported that they were serving in pastoral ministry. Twenty-one women listed their occupation as "homemaker," while many more listed no occupation at all. While recognizing that choosing full-time family as a career is a legitimate choice for these women, we can also see the influence of the colleges in these choices.

One female faculty member tried to organize a lecture series for female students interested in pursuing careers in the ministry. She intended to bring female pastors and seminary professors to campus to talk to the young women but was told by her department that they would fund the series only if she included homemakers as a professional ministry and invited full-time homemakers to come to talk about what they do.

According to historian Margaret Bendroth, this drive to steer women away from careers represents a late-twentieth-century innovation, rather than "traditionalism." Bendroth gives evidence that women were widely recruited to fill many positions in full-time fundamentalist Christian ministry during the first half of the twentieth century, and she argues that "through the 1940s fundamentalist women shared, and even surpassed, the national trend toward female employment after World War I." Worldly women worked for "pin money," but Christian women worked to further God's Kingdom. According to Bendroth, the fundamentalist John R. Rice, the author of many books that advocated women's submission, including *Bobbed Hair, Bossy Wives, and Women Preachers*, discouraged his own daughter from settling for a life as the wife of a banker because she had been "trained for full-time Christian service."[13] Women report suffering from a pervasive fear that if they pursue careers as professionals, they are consigning themselves to lives of singleness. The subculture has subtly taught them that if they are too successful, no man will ever want to marry them. A female seminary student and award-winning preacher told me,

> I've thought about this as I've been invited to preach in different churches and they always say, "Will you be bringing someone with you?" . . . And I always say no. And I started thinking I probably will *never* have a significant other who's going to want to go with me when I preach sermons because that's not what I've been taught how women are supposed to relate. I'm supposed to be going with *him* while *he's* preaching. (emphasis in original)

Despite the earlier emphasis placed on the significance of the work of women, young women now in Christian colleges report feeling undermined by their professors, and they struggle to describe experiences that are subtle and hard to document:

> My painful experience came mostly in the form of what was not said, what was not addressed, and what was not challenged. . . . While the experience of structural discrimination, in this case gender based, is concrete, the relaying of it seems inconclusive and feels suspect for lack of substance.

General attitudes in favor of women's submissiveness, passivity, and silence subtly discourage women from seeking leadership positions. Women are frequently told they ask too many questions.

> You're just [considered] a troublemaker. And I've had people that I don't know remember me from class as the person who asked all those questions. And I ask very few questions. I might ask, at the most, once a week I might ask a question. Probably not even that often—I think it's because I'm one of the only women that asks questions.

And while young men who discern a call to the ministry are nurtured and mentored immediately, women who discern such a call often feel that they get little support from their larger community. One woman who had won a prestigious preaching award at her seminary had been asked to preach at a nearby church. There were some last-minute mix-ups, and in the end she had only a short time to organize the service. It didn't go well, and she was "humiliated."

> I didn't have the experience to just go in and "wing it." And then, when the service started falling apart, I didn't have enough experience to know how to just change gears and fix it. And then I started thinking that this was just the fourth time I had preached in a church. Whereas with men, when they would win a preaching award, they'd probably been preaching for several years because as soon as they get called to ministry, their church probably gives them an opportunity to preach. And so they have experience before they win awards. They win awards, I guess because they have experience. But yet women—we get our experience because we've already won an award.

Instead of being supported in their callings, women report being met with suspicion and hostility. "I realized that [because I am a woman] . . . I would be assumed to be a radical, lesbian, post-Christian who worked academically from an emotionally based perspective until proven otherwise."

Being one of only a few women, or even the only woman, in a class can be intimidating to women, especially in a setting where they perceive a lack of support from their male colleagues. At one school, a woman told me about an American church history class in which she was one of two women. On the first day, she timidly sat off to one side alone; thereafter, she and the other woman sat together every class period. There were two men in the class who she believed were hostile to the presence of women in seminary, and throughout the term she was bothered by their mumbled comments and ridiculing laughter. At one point, when the professor was out of town and a graduate student was substituting for him, the class covered the topic of Anne Hutchinson and her expulsion from Massachusetts. The two male students joked and ridiculed Hutchinson the entire class period. At first the two female students thought they were probably being overly sensitive, but the next day, with the same graduate student teaching, the topic was Roger Williams, and the young men were very serious.[14] In telling me the story, the woman asked rhetorically,

> Why is it a joke when we study—the only time we ever study women in church is just basically when there is a joke? And then why was it funny when she got kicked out of Massachusetts but it was really sad when Roger Williams was sent out?

According to the woman I talked with, these same male students made relentless jokes about witches, laughing about burning them and saying that there were a few witches in their own churches they would like to burn.

While these female students are frustrated and angry when fellow students show disrespect for women, they are devastated when that disrespect comes from the professors, who are so greatly revered. Speaking about the members of the faculty in her religious studies department, one particularly articulate woman said,

> There was an assumption that women would not be serious scholars. . . . There was an assumption that men had power and value, granted and sustained by our biblical text, and that women only had access to those

things through the controlling discernment of men. There was an assumption that the objectification of women's bodies and devaluation of women's minds was "natural" and indeed partially desirable to women. These assumptions acted as silent boundaries that intuitively told women where their value lay and made any woman suspect who dare [*sic*] venture out of the prescribed expectations.

The young women report feeling like outsiders in class; they believe that women's participation in class was devalued; and they were chagrined when "stereotypes about women's mental capacities and personhood [were] joked about by students and unchallenged by the professor." When one woman decided to declare her major, she said she was "filled with fear and insecurity." She said she had known of other women who had gone to her department to declare themselves religious studies majors and had been "blatantly challenged by the questioning of their intellectual ability."[15] Another woman told of an incident in a language class in which she indicated she was having difficulty understanding something. According to this woman, the professor responded to her, in front of the class, by saying, "Have you ever considered the possibility that you might be stupid?" This same woman reported that this same professor discouraged her from attending graduate school by telling her, "You'll meet someone and get married and forget all about grad school." He also once called her "butch" because she had cut her hair short and told students that one of his colleagues would never be happy with her professional accomplishments because she was not married.

On the other hand, the women with whom I spoke all shared stories of support and affirmation, as well as stories of discouragement. In every instance, there were a few people who had sparked their interest and many more who were neither instrumental in their growth nor a detriment to it. Young women who perceive a call on their lives from God and then face conflicting messages about its legitimacy often find that the single most important factor in determining whether they pursue that call is the availability of supportive mentors.

I approached the question with fear for I held my tradition and faith incredibly valuable to me. Yet I felt a conflict with who I was and what I was called to do. It was not until I had a class with Dr. Brown that the full weight [of my calling] was made known to me. Sitting in her class I saw, for the first time, my own potential for further study. In her academic excellence, religious faithfulness, and passionate teaching I began to see a path which was simultaneously authentic to my person as a woman and to the faith of my tradition.

The female students all agreed that they desperately needed more mentors but that in the existing circumstances those mentors were hard to find. Sharply delineated gender boundaries made it difficult for male professors to mentor female students. Men felt they could not be alone with a single women without giving the impression of impropriety. Furthermore, the very small number of female faculty members, combined with the large numbers of female students, made it unlikely that many female students would have an opportunity to be mentored by women.[16]

Despite the fact that parents send their children (especially their daughters) to Christian colleges to preserve their innocence, at each institution I found stories of sexual violation and date rape. The women who told me these stories claimed that, even when they reported the incidences, they were often hushed up and little was done about them. Students in one situation speculated that their school could not afford to do anything too public about charges of date rape made against one young man by fifteen women. The woman I interviewed had also had a problem with this young man that she did not report.

> I mean, economically, you know, our parents are not going to want to spend thousands of dollars to protect their little virginous [sic] daughters at this college, you know, if they think they are going to get raped and assaulted.

Another young woman I interviewed had agreed to help a fellow student with a photography project for his communications class. In addition to being a student, the young man was also employed as a security guard for the school. The photo session took place in the library and required a change of clothes. The woman claimed that the young man had set up a camera in the dressing room and was filming his photo subjects as they changed and that she was one of several victims. The young man later "confessed" to the school counselor that he was addicted to pornography. The women were informed that he had taken the photos, but he was not removed from his position, nor was he required to leave the school. The young women claimed that they were never presented with the option of pursuing further action against him and were even discouraged from doing so. The school's interest in keeping the incident quiet furthered the injury to the victims by contributing to their feelings of powerlessness.

> [Everyone] told me I was just making too big an issue out of it. . . . I wish I would have made a bigger issue out of it. I would feel better about myself right now if I had done something about it. If I could do it over again I would have pressed charges irregardless [*sic*] of what the school did.

In another case, a young man had been accused of date rape; according to my respondent, fifteen female students came forward to testify against him with similar accusations. The woman I interviewed (who was one of only a few outspoken feminists on her campus) claimed that the young man had never been charged because the young woman who initially accused him was viewed as "kind of like a slut." She emphasized that this was not her view but the view she believed the administration took. In the end, she said, the school allowed the young man to return, despite the many accusations against him and, apparently, a prior dismissal from a job in a parachurch ministry for the same problem.

In another case on the same campus, the son of a rather prominent administrator was accused of repeatedly raping a girl who was too intimidated to report it. The accused held a part-time job on campus and was allowed to remain because the victim would not bring charges.

Understanding the cultural context in which these incidences took place is a necessary prerequisite to appreciating their significance. These are college-age women who have been raised with a tremendous emphasis on modesty. They dress very conservatively and take their sexual purity extremely seriously. Many of them are virgins, and almost all of them would claim to be. Having their sexuality deprivatized in these ways is particularly humiliating for them. Because purity is so essential to being "Christian," unwanted sexual attention undermines not only their sense of self but also their sense of their relationship with God.

> I just felt like I walked around with this sexual sensuality. Something that oozed from me. . . . I felt like I wasn't a good Christian. I must, um, maybe I'm not dressing appropriately. Yet I always made a point of dressing very professionally.

Like most institutions where men and women with drastically different levels of power spend significant amounts of time together, there are instances of sexual harassment. When sexual harassment occurs in religious institutions, however, the harassment and its implications for the victims take on some unique characteristics.[17]

For the most part, the harassment about which I was told was much milder in form than what might be found in a secular context. None of it resulted in sexual intercourse, and in fact it might more precisely be labeled gendered intimidation. Despite the seeming mildness of the harassment, however, its power to undermine the self-confidence of the victims is magnified by the context. In fact, the oft-cited notion that sexual harassment is more about power than it is about sex is demonstrated with clarity in these situations.

One woman attended a school beach party wearing "the most conservative two-piece bathing suit" she could find. Modesty is important in the conservative Christian world, and her intention was to avoid drawing undue attention to herself, especially unwanted sexual attention. A week later, at another event at which there was a receiving line, the president of the college joked that the faculty had decided to put her on the cover of its next publication wearing what she had worn at the beach party. She was angered by this comment from a man she expected to be able to see her in terms of her academic achievements and not as a sex object. Then, a few days later, she met with two female faculty members to discuss her thesis, which was a study of the treatment of women in her religious community. She was about to use the story of the president's comment to illustrate the kinds of issues that would shape her study when one of the professors interrupted her to say, with raised eyebrows, that everyone knew about her bathing suit. She was devastated and told me:

> I just started to cry. That the faculty that were at this beach party—and some of them had wives with them—were like little boys who saw someone in a swim suit and ran back to the other faculty and said—you know—I could just hear them, they had this conversation about me and my body. . . . I felt like, for people called into certain positions of leadership in a Christian context, [they] had a responsibility to maintain very appropriate lines of behavior. I don't care if they thought I was attractive. I don't care.

In another case, a professor was eventually let go (without public explanation) after students complained over several years about subtle improprieties, including ambiguous touching and gender-based emotional manipulation. The professor was known for pointing out that female students were infatuated with him and "admitted," both in public and apparently in private with students, that he "lusted after" his female students.[18] At least one female student interpreted this "admission" as an invitation. It's impossible to understand the perceived manipulation of such an "invitation" without coming to terms with the authority of a man in this position in the subculture. As a Bible professor who worked with the ancient text in the original languages, he was known as an authority both on campus and in the larger community and was highly esteemed; he was described to me as being "intimidatingly god-like."

Feminists have long argued that abuse of power and the manipulation are at the root of sexual harassment and even rape and that such violations are more about power than they are about sex. That many women have understood these situations as abuses of power and as sexual manipulation, even when no overt sex was involved, and that they have perceived such violations as pervasive problems resulting from underlying cultural notions about the nature of men and women points to their importance in conflict over the power to produce culture.[19]

The Fallout

The views of many women leaders in both the ministry and the academy on the proper roles of men and women have evolved over time. Early in their adult lives, they often agree with the so-called traditionalist teaching that women should submit to men, that husbands are the heads of their families, and that women were created to take a subordinate role. As they come to embrace evangelical feminism and try to reshape their lives to fit their growing understanding of "Christian liberty" as it applies to women, they find themselves in increasingly difficult situations. As early as 1979, Virginia Hearn edited an evangelical feminist volume that explores the stories of women who were on this journey of understanding. Entitled *Our Struggle to Serve: The Stories of 15 Evangelical Women,*[20] Hearn's work is intended for a popular evangelical audience accustomed to light devotional reading. While the essays do, indeed, discuss moments of pain and self-doubt, profound moments of discouragement, and even divorce, they only scratch the surface of the anguish and turmoil created by this worldview shift.

Because these issues impact the work lives, home lives, and spiritual lives of these women, many find that, at the same time they are facing conflicts in their jobs, their marriages are falling apart and their spiritual lives are a shambles. At its best, evangelical patriarchy is put forth as a gentle, loving leadership, but at its worst it can be the justification for abuse.[21] One woman reports that in her young marriage her husband "frequently" warned her that he could tell God not to listen to her prayers "and God would cut her off."[22] One of my interview subjects told me how her husband's anger increased in proportion to her increasing independence and how he was inclined to fly into a rage at a moment's notice. She began to label his behavior abusive but soon realized that she did not have the option of leaving. While no longer financially dependent on him, she knew that, because the emotional abuse had left no visible scars, she would not be able to justify a divorce and would, therefore, lose her job.

> If I left, where was I to go? The church wasn't going to support me. I'd be a divorced woman. My parents weren't going to support me because I had committed the ultimate sin by divorcing my husband. In evangelical culture—besides lesbianism and homosexuality—divorce in *the* unforgivable sin.

The closer this woman examined the teachings of her religious tradition regarding women, the more she came to believe that "God hates women." In trying to reconcile the person she believed herself to be and the requirements of the God she knew, she told me, in the most tearful of my interviews,

> Everything I did within the church would be a sin because of the fact that I am a woman—if I was to express what I was in the church. And so I come back to this theology that is taught at [my seminary] that God is a man. And that is really the way they teach it. God is not a man! But it's taught as though God is a man so therefore anything that is not male cannot please God. And pleasing God was the one thing I wanted to do so I was put in an impossible spot. Woman are not important to God. Unless their role is to make sure that men's socks are sorted and their meals are on the table. Oh, and they can play the piano on Sunday mornings. But women in their fullness separate from men cannot please God.

What she perceived as a cruel cosmic joke led her to question her faith altogether. She talked of her "theological underpinnings" falling apart:

> I began to question everything and I kept trying to just patch it. It's like, you know, patching this dike. And I kept trying and trying and saying, you know, "this is really okay, this is really okay." And "I'm just misunderstanding here." And finally I had to say: "It's gone." I guess I couldn't keep patching any longer.

Most of the time she sat in class (she was a seminary student at the time) believing that she "had no theology," at times saying, "I don't even believe in God any longer—I just didn't have anything to stand on any longer."

> And this is when things began to get really rocky with the marriage because when I tried to talk to my husband about this, and he was still in this very rigid thinking mode where life is clear: this is good, and this is bad, and there's nothing in between. He was horrified by the fact that I would even suggest that I was struggling with my belief structure. So I quit talking to him about it.

Even women who don't experience this kind of existential crisis of faith often find it difficult to continue in fellowship in an evangelical church since so few recognize women's calling to leadership. One woman told me of a friend who had recently moved to Colorado Springs.

> They visited seven churches over the last seven or eight months, trying to find a church where she could worship and feel a valid part of the congregation. And they have not been able to find one.

The significance of this becomes clear when we realize that membership (and even leadership) in a local church is often a criterion for evaluation in hiring and tenure review processes. Many women report resorting to extensive therapy and even antidepressant drugs to muddle through these difficult times.

> I actually do feel better right at the moment, I feel mentally and emotionally better than I have felt in a long time. But I know it's purely chemical because none of my problems are solved. Nothing has been dealt with.

The only relief is that for the first time I'm considering leaving [this school], which is something I just couldn't do before.

Isn't This the Same Everywhere?

Because these women's stories reminded me of issues raised and conflicts faced by feminists who were making inroads in a variety of spheres, I specifically asked my respondents whether they thought their situations were unique and, if so, how they were so. One woman explained,

> Well, I think there is sexism everywhere, granted, but when you just look at the sheer numbers. I mean, the fact that in out of ninety schools I am one of only two women [who hold the position I hold] and among the Christian College Coalition member schools only 19 percent of the senior positions are filled by women. And that hasn't changed. I've been tracking it every year for six years. So we are worse than our secular counterparts.

Women in Christian higher education do face one major difference: that which would be called sexism in a secular context is often seen as being endorsed by God in a religious context. A female seminary professor expressed this well when she told me about a survey that had been done on her campus concerning attitudes toward racism and sexism. She believes her campus is in the process of coming to grips with its own racism and recognizing it as sin, but there is no such recognition with regard to sexism:

> There's a lot of talk about sensitivity, you know, how to work with our cultural differences. And as they talked I realized that, as a campus, we would come to grips with the racial issues, the multicultural issues, because we are very multicultural and this is important. But, we will never come to grips with the gender issues because they feel *biblically* justified in their attitudes. . . . They feel like they can always justify a more demeaning stance toward women.

Beth, a faculty member at another institution, confirmed this, saying,

> And I know when I hear from women from secular schools, it's not easy. But it's almost easier to handle because it's not cloaked in some sort of

theological language. I mean, it's just blatant sexism, and you can confront it as blatant sexism. But in our schools you can't call it sin, because it's seen as almost righteous, pious. . . . And we wouldn't sue, I mean because that's just not a Christian thing to do.

This belief that it is "not Christian" to sue another believer is based on an argument made in I Corinthians 7:6. The Apostle Paul writes that Christians should not go before civil courts with their disputes because it will bring dishonor to their community; it is inappropriate because ultimately Christians will judge the angels and should, therefore, be able to settle their own disputes among themselves.

In addition to feeling that they do not have the option of suing over sex discrimination, women also feel as if other potential remedies are closed off by the uniqueness of their situation. Since questions about the roles of women are theological ones, even organizations that claim to support women in leadership are often unwilling to require a commitment to women in leadership on the part of everyone in the organization; it's seen as a point of religious liberty. So women who do manage to work their way into positions of responsibility often bemoan a perceived lack of support from their superiors. One woman explained that at her most recent job, many of her peers had resented her presence:

And the president didn't do anything to validate my position. And he would sort of send me out to do something but [the others] knew they didn't have to do anything that I asked them to do and they knew the president wouldn't do anything about it if they didn't. So it made my job really hard. I had to spend a lot of time and energy sort of trying to coax them—but in the end, if they wouldn't help me—they knew there were no consequences.

Even in positions where women feel some real support from their immediate supervisors, this perceived inability to require support from others in the institution is a persistent problem:

He lets male members of my staff go around me and go straight to him and he'll promise them things or he'll sort of agree with them that I'm sort of a little bitch. . . . And when I've confronted him on that he goes: "Oh yeah, I know I shouldn't do that" but then the next time they're back in his office again and he's promising them things.

Because evangelicals see clearly the role of Christian institutions in shaping the subculture for the years to come, questions over how women may function in them take on great significance. The problems outlined in this chapter contribute to the production of an environment that is often inhospitable to women. Since only small numbers of women successfully negotiate the course of academic achievement and promotion, there are, in turn, fewer women to serve as mentors to female students in Christian colleges and seminaries.

PART II

Analysis and Interpretation

In Part I, we looked at case studies to explore some of the parameters and dimensions of gender culture in conservative American Protestantism. We saw that, despite the way conservative Protestants are typically portrayed, norms and expectations concerning women and women's roles in this world are not fixed, static, and monolithic; on the contrary, they are in a state of constant change. We picked up our examination of the process of that change at a particular point in history (with the rise of biblical feminism in the 1970s) and explored the ways in which biblical feminists have worked to transform the subculture according to their views. We then looked at Southern Seminary as an example of the ways in which traditionalists sought to change the subculture again by securing a return to their own views—albeit a version of their views that was informed by the changes brought by the biblical feminists. Part I concluded with a survey of the individual war stories of women in leadership positions in this conservative Christian world.

I have argued that, in neglecting the variety of voices in the conservative Christian world, in attempting to construct a coherent narrative, we have missed much of what these stories can tell us about the making of a religious subculture. With that in mind, we now move to Part II, the goal of which is to explore exactly these questions: What do we now know about women in this conservative Christian world that we didn't know before? And, more broadly, what does what we now know about the women tell us about the conservative Christian world itself?

4

Theoretical Issues

Scholars have documented the significance of gender as an organizing issue for fundamentalism. An important example of the focus on antifeminism as central to fundamentalism is Betty DeBerg's *Ungodly Women: Gender and the First Wave of American Fundamentalism.* DeBerg argues that the "origins and urgency of fundamentalism . . . [can be traced to] the drastic changes in gender ideology and behavior between 1880 and 1930."[1] Hers was the first study to look at the significance of gender for the development of fundamentalism in America. DeBerg convincingly argues that fear over rapidly changing roles for men and women and the increasing feminization of religion generally contributed to the crystallization of fundamentalist opposition to modernity. That this remained true of conservative Protestantism at the end of the twentieth century is evidenced by the focus of the religious right on gender-related issues including women's rights abortion, and gay rights.

We have seen that the scholarship on conservative religious women has also evolved over time to include an increasing level of complexity and nuance, documenting both an essentially antifeminist strain of conservative Protestantism and a strongly feminist one.

Often, studies do not examine issues of gender specifically but make references to it within larger explorations of conservative Protestantism's conflict with modernity. In *Baptist Battles,* Nancy Ammerman examines the fight for control of the Southern Baptist Convention and shows that changing gender roles continue to have a crystallizing influence on Protestant fundamentalists.[2] In Ammerman's study, the issue of women's ordination (instead of the inerrancy of the Bible) often served as the litmus test by which Baptists discerned which side a person had chosen in recent Baptist controversies between moderates and fundamentalists.[3]

But, because current work tends not to explore discrepancies between ideology and practice, and because it tends to try to smooth over conflicting aspects to develop a coherent narrative, it often ends up missing the story of the ongoing conflict over gender ideology within the movements, thereby also missing the opportunity to theorize about conflict as a key element in the process of cultural production and reproduction.

A few studies of gender in conservative Christianity do draw out the alternative perspectives within the tradition; these scholars explore the departures from conservative norms in both practice and ideology and examine the growing feminist movement within the conservative Protestant culture. Thus, more nuanced portrayals of conservative Protestant gender ideology and practice do exist and are becoming increasingly common. For example, in his 1987 book *Evangelicalism: The Coming Generation,* James Davison Hunter documents the existence and influence of a feminist movement within conservative Protestantism.[4] Hunter interviewed future leaders of evangelicalism at evangelical colleges and seminaries and found that, while they frequently rejected the label "feminist," their convictions and biblical interpretations had been greatly influenced by the biblical feminist movement. Many of those who promote these views, however, do identify themselves as feminists. Calling themselves Christian feminists, biblical feminists, or evangelical feminists, they advocate women's equality in marriage, women's ordination, complete equality in all Christian ministry, and the use of gender-inclusive language in liturgy, hymnody, theology, and even biblical translation.

Judith Stacey gave life to Hunter's numbers by interviewing female evangelicals who have feminist sympathies. In *Brave New Families,* Stacey gives an ethnographic report of an evangelical woman who has incorporated biblical feminism into her version of evangelicalism.[5] In "'We Are Not Doormats': The Influence of Feminism on Contemporary Evangelicals in the United States," she and Elizabeth Susan Gerard "examin[e] the diffusion" of feminist ideas within evangelical Christianity.[6] They review evangelical feminist literature and report on interviews with evangelical feminist women. But, like many scholars, Stacy and Gerard see the evangelical feminists as an example of conservative Protestant accommodation to the larger culture, rather than recognizing them as part of a longstanding tradition within evangelicalism and fundamentalism. Rather than taking seriously the alternative views that are present in those traditions, they explain such variations as "accommodation" to the larger culture. Stacey and Gerard write that evangelicalism "selectively incorporates and adapts many feminist family reforms." And, as feminists, the authors conclude that there has been "extraordinary diffusion of *our* influence on even this most unlikely of constituents" (emphasis added). They confess that they were "surprised" to find a "feminist consciousness" among some evangelicals.[7] And yet, there are several historical treatments of gender in fundamentalism and evangelicalism that show that there have long been supporters of women's equality within these traditions; indeed, the feminist movement itself came out of nineteenth century evangelical reform movements.[8] But notions of accommodation and assimilation require the assumption of a fixed standard to which a movement or group being studied can be compared. Instead, I propose that doing justice to the conflicting voices in the conservative Christian world leads us to see that there is no fixed gender that exists independent of culture, waiting to be transformed by accommodation to other cultural forces. On the contrary, gender in this world (as in others, I suspect) is the product of ongoing cultural work characterized by negotiation, compromise, and even conflict. When we recognize that the gendered requirements, expectations, and limitations in the evangelical subculture are the result of ongoing conflict, we can look at culture as something that is explicitly produced, rather than as the implicit backdrop against which life occurs, and then look for the ways in which this occurs.

Cultural Production Theory

The sociology of religion has recently emphasized issues related to the "production of culture."[9] Production-of-culture models emphasize the institutions and resources that participate in the process of the production of culture, such as people, financial means, organizations, training, and so forth, as well as the role played by the audiences for that which is produced.[10]

Robert Wuthnow lays out the various dimensions of this approach to studying religion, which he calls the "new cultural sociology."[11]

> Rather than thinking of culture as something implicit or taken for granted . . . the new cultural sociology regards culture as something tangible, explicit, overtly produced. It consists of texts, discourse, language, music, and the symbolic-expressive dimensions of interpersonal behavior, and so on. Proponents of this view hold that any specific cultural artifact

should be examined in terms of questions about its production, its relation with other cultural elements, its internal structure, and the resources that determine how well it becomes institutionalized.[12]

Wuthnow points to three groups of issues that arise from this new approach to studying culture. First, the focus on the production of culture leads us to pay attention to the "internal structure of culture itself," to take symbols seriously in and of themselves. Symbols are not to be understood merely for the meaning individuals attach to them but themselves become the object of study: "The true object of analysis is symbolism itself, not just the meanings that subjects attach to it."[13] This approach to the study of religion relies on analysis of "observable cultural materials: texts, sermons, and discourse," rather than the "subjective consciousness" of individuals.[14]

This is a significant departure from the more traditional way of looking at religion as an integrated worldview, and this new approach yields a picture of religion that is characterized by "discrete statements or tenets" that can be "combined flexibly with other tenets." Wuthnow even uses the term "hodge-podge" to describe the picture that emerges from this type of analysis.[15]

The second group of issues that Wuthnow raises pertains to the ways in which the dimensions of culture are enacted and lived out. This social dimension of culture "dramatizes something about social relations. It tells people how to behave in relation to one another, thereby creating a kind of moral order among them."[16]

The final group of issues to which Wuthnow points are those related to the institutions that produce culture. Here he focuses on questions about resources, access to power, and so forth, playing up intentionality and calculation. Culture seems to result from the interaction between the elites and the people in the pews. In an almost dispassionate and businesslike manner, elites make decisions about the allocation of resources, always motivated to garner resources for their own enterprises, while the people in the pews receive the produced culture and mold it to fit into their own lives.

Conflict Theory

Recent work in religious studies has shifted from the institutional negotiation of resources and power to out-and-out conflict over the right to interpret and control the sacred, which is the dimension of culture with which Wuthnow is concerned. This perspective is most clearly set forth in the theoretical introduction to *American Sacred Space*, edited by David Chidester and Edward T. Linenthal.[17] Chidester and Linenthal present two trajectories of analysis of the sacred within the field of religious studies. In the poetics of the sacred, based in the work of scholars like Mircea Eliade, the sacred is perceived as "an uncanny, awesome, powerful manifestation of reality, full of ultimate significance."[18] In this poetics of the sacred, scholars looked for manifestations, intrusions into the mundane world, awesome experiences of the sacred, which were perceived as an external force existing autonomously, waiting to be "discovered." The alternative understanding, which Chidester and Linenthal label the politics of the sacred, explores the cultural work that produces the sacred. They argue that an essential quality (perhaps *the* essential quality) of the sacred is its contestedness.[19]

This contestedness is nowhere more discernable than in the study of sacred space. As Chidester and Linenthal argue, sacred space is "ritual space, a location for formalized repeatable symbolic performances,"[20] a "site, orientation, or set of relations subject to interpretation because it focuses crucial questions about what it means to be human in a meaningful world,"[21] and, finally, "contested space, a site of negotiated contests over the legitimate ownership of sacred symbols."[22] They note the decentered nature of sacred space in the context of postmodernity, recognizing that there is no overriding myth that gives the space called "America" a unified meaning.

In the immediacy of a modern subjectivity, as mediated, however, through distinctive narrative strategies, or, more often, as fragmented and multiplied under the effects of modernity, American sacred space has been rediscovered as mobile and pluriform, harrowing, yet still perhaps hallowed, suggesting a mythic orientation that is not securely anchored in a stable sacred landscape but is at risk in a modern world of media and mobility.[23]

Sociologists, too, have stepped up their interest in conflict. James Davison Hunter's work *Culture Wars* has framed much of the current debate among sociologists of religion.[24] Hunter argues that there is a cultural divide in American public life that there exist two "general public philosophies" that are grounded in different sources of moral authority and are at odds over basic issues such as the meanings of freedom and justice. He names these two visions for America "progressivist" and "orthodox." Given that the title of his subsequent work is *Before the Shooting Begins*, he is not terribly hopeful about the possibilities of a meeting of the minds between the two camps.[25] Some scholars take Hunter to task for fostering division.[26] Others argue that the evidence does not support a theory based on two clearly delineated sides.[27] Example after example is cited in which this group or that group defies the model. Critics argue that people do not embrace political agendas as a whole but rather pick and choose from among alternatives.[28] They argue that, although elites may be caught up in a culture war, the ideological convictions of most Americans are more accurately pictured as a pastiche of attitudes and perceptions grounded in the more practical need to negotiate the issues faced in everyday life, than a systematic ideological vision created with a concern for consistency.

Hunter replies to these critics by pointing out that the existence of competing moral visions that are the source of cultural conflict is not dependent on the ideological consistency of individual "people's attitudes about public issues."[29]

Still others argue that the cultural battles are more often within traditions than between them.[30] On the basis of their study of seminary contexts, Jackson W. Carroll and Penny Long Marler have found evidence for the argument that whatever "culture war" exists is *within* liberal and conservative organizations, rather than *between* them. The conflict within the evangelical feminist movement at CBE would seem to fit their argument. What was, in many ways, the defining moment for the movement was not the result of conflict generated by "traditionalists" but instead a disagreement with other evangelical feminists.[31]

The culture wars model is also problematic because it is linear and unidimensional. Much of the debate challenging the "two-party theory" has focused on whether we can say there is a third possibility: a center. Clearly, CBE has worked hard to hold a middle ground between more liberal and more conservative factions within the conservative Protestant movement. But the fault lines in these conflicts run in many more directions than this model represents; biblical feminists are "conservative" on some issues and "liberal" on others. Biblical feminists, and CBE, have even managed to stake out positions that bring together liberalism and conservatism on still other issues. They are not just in the middle. Their views have been well received in the subculture and have grown increasingly influential. At the same time, however, polarizing forces have wrought havoc. The effort to maintain legitimacy in the eyes of other evangelicals has required biblical feminists to expend significant energy demonstrating that biblical feminism is not necessarily a threat to the evangelical ordering of reality that is grounded in gendered dualism. We need a multidimensional model that can account for these various cleavages and alliances.

If conflict is an essential category for the analysis of cultural production, a religious subculture may be an ideal place to study it. As Hunter and Sargeant have argued, conflict in the context of American religion has more significance than we might realize. Americans may be less inclined to look toward religious institutions to guide their behavior than they were a generation ago, but religion, broadly defined, is still a powerful force in the lives of individuals. It is often in these religious institutions that "matters of moral authority are *directly* hammered out, challenged and bargained over." And, as Hunter and Sargeant argue, the fallout from these battles fought in the context of religion often spill over into the discourse of the larger culture.[32]

Gender Theory

In her book *Gender Trouble: Feminism and the Subversion of Identity*,[33] Judith Butler offers at least three insights that have informed my analysis. First, as she explores the mechanisms by which gender is constructed, Butler demonstrates the ways in which oppositional movements depend upon, and replicate, the structures they oppose. Her critique of notions of "essential" femininity creates a space for alternative versions of "woman" that include, at once, both lesbians and conservative women.

Second, Butler develops a "performative" theory of gender to explore what I have called a dialectic in the production of gender culture:

> In this sense, *gender* is not a noun, but neither is it a set of free floating attributes, for we have seen that the substantive effect of gender is performatively produced and compelled by the regulatory practices of gender coherence. . . . There is no gender identity behind the expressions of gender; that identity is performatively constituted by the very "expressions" that are said to be its results.[34]

Third, throughout the book, Butler echoes many scholars of culture when she argues that the most effective mechanisms for producing gender (or culture) are those that are most effectively concealed.

Gender as a Contested Category

This book draws these theoretical perspectives together. While the focus on the production of culture clearly has merit, the picture that emerges from Wuthnow's discussion of that production is much too neat and clean; it is almost sanitized.[35] In the trenches, the actual production of culture is the result of serious ongoing conflict; it often more closely resembles a street fight than a corporate board meeting. While important, Wuthnow's emphasis on the availability and allocation of resources misses the turmoil and destruction that find their way into the lives of those who are engaged in the process of producing culture "on the ground." I emphasize the conflict involved in the production of gender as a central element, and a key cultural symbol, of a religious culture.

While I assume the existence and power of patriarchy, in showing ongoing conflict I seek to push beyond it to examine various dimensions of the production of a symbol that is both religious and cultural. It is not enough to show the production of gender ideology as the imposition of the views of a more powerful group upon a less powerful group. Gender is evolving and malleable and at least partly explicitly produced and reproduced.

Attempts to find a middle ground between feminists and traditionalists notwithstanding, these ways of understanding and ordering reality are profoundly different, and, when they vie for hegemony, tremendous conflict ensues. This is not to argue that everyone is part of the battle; many people are not. Yet, in evangelicalism's internecine battles, gender is an important dimension of the conflict and often the dividing line that separates one constituency from another.

Alternative viewpoints and creative blending notwithstanding, the traditionalists have been the dominant voice in the conservative Christian debate over gender. Throughout the 1970s and 1980s, the feminists gained something of a foothold in the seminaries and colleges. But, while they had an impact on many future leaders, they failed to transform the entire subculture. Feminist perspectives were incorporated into the worldview and theology, but at the popular level, traditionalism, and the gendered dualism that is at the heart of its worldview, retained its hold.

This tenacity results, in part, from the fact that, while feminists concentrated their efforts almost exclusively at the rhetorical and ideological level, traditionalist were adept at representing and replicating their view of reality in other aspects of culture. What follows is an examination of the processes by which traditionalists reproduced their view of reality in the context of material culture and the little details of everyday life.

Resources for Cultural Production

Within the evangelical subculture, the opponents of hierarchical gender roles have largely abandoned the power of material culture to the proponents of traditional ideology. The evidence of conflict seen in other dimensions of the culture is absent here. Evangelical feminists expend most of their energy and resources fighting institutional and theological battles, but dualistic constructions of gender are more readily represented materially than are fluid constructions that emphasize equality. While there is evidence that evangelical feminists have gained significant ground on the institutional and theological fronts,[36] the fact remains that gendered dualism is perpetuated on a popular level by virtue of the fact that the material culture that gives shape to everyday life reproduces it.

There are, of course, forces that mitigate against traditionalism—not the least of which are the attitudes and expectations of the larger culture of which evangelicals are also a part. The history of evangelical support for women's equality is also important.

Because scholars have emphasized the theological and intellectual aspects of conservative Christianity to the exclusion of cultural aspects, they have failed to capture what I contend is its essential nature. By looking at the material culture that evangelicals produce, we can discern a much overlooked dimension of who these people are. The culture they have produced is profoundly gendered, suggesting that evangelicalism, as a religious movement, is itself essentially gendered. As we move from this discussion of material culture to our subsequent exploration of other dimensions of the evangelical culture—discourse, practice, norms, and behavioral expectations—we find increasing levels of conflict, negotiation, and compromise. Wuthnow argues that scholars need to focus on the *content* of discourse, as well as on "discourse in practice."[37] He criticizes traditional sociological approaches that reduce efforts to find meaning in life to the products of educational levels or social status: "We should also seek to know what is said."[38] What follows is an examination of "what is said" by evangelicals about gender and an exploration of how what is said is incorporated into the lives of believers. It is drawn from a combination of primary-source documents and interviews.

* 5 *

The Power of Subtle Arrangements
and Little Things

The argument that gender is constructed and that there are specific cultural mechanisms that produce it begs the question as to the mechanisms by which this happens. In Chapter 2, we looked at the ways that biblical feminists sought to bring their conservative Christian world into line with their views and at some of the compromises they made to ensure that they could protect their ability to speak as insiders and to maintain a level of legitimacy. This chapter, on the other hand, looks at some of the cultural mechanism used to reproduce gendered dualism and what proponents call traditionalism.

Michel Foucault has observed that since the seventeenth century, religious institutions, like prisons and the military, have been preoccupied with "small acts of cunning," "subtle arrangements," "detailed characteristics," and "little things."[1] Foucault draws our attention to the power of the seemingly insignificant.

The gender-based culture of evangelicals and fundamentalists is produced and replicated by such "subtle arrangements" and "little things"—small behavioral requirements that serve to create and to perpetuate gender segregation and a gendered social hierarchy.

These often unspoken behavioral rules and requirements are harder to document than the gendered nature of the material or ideological dimensions of culture, and they are particularly difficult for critics within the tradition to challenge because such criticism is made to seem petty. Furthermore, they are often such an accepted part of everyday life that the degree to which they are part of the production of gendered culture is often overlooked. But there can be no doubt these "little things" are, in reality, very powerful.

Small Group Meetings

Small group meetings, home church meetings, or discipleship groups are increasingly popular in growing evangelical churches.[2] These typically gender-segregated groups often serve as the backbone of these churches. Anyone who wishes to be included among the "core" members of the church is expected to attend one of these weekly group meetings—and probably eventually to lead one.

The women's groups commonly discuss problems related to family and home and to the difficulty of balancing work demands with family demands, the assumption being that the woman's primary calling is to her family. Single women in these groups are encouraged to "wait on the Lord" for providing a mate or to learn to accept singleness if that is "God's plan," with the assumption always being that singleness is something of a defective state. They talk about depression and recovery, relationships and home management. The underlying assumption is usually that women are either at home raising families or are striving to attain that status. Bible teaching at these meetings is usually devotional in style, emphasizing feeling close to God and being led by Him.[3]

The teaching at men's meetings, on the other hand, often focuses on theology or practical application of biblical texts to daily life. Men are constantly encouraged to seek leadership positions both in the church and in their families. The integration of Christian faith with business is a frequent topic, as is men's personal problems with issues like pornography and marital infidelity.

In addition to weekly meetings or Bible studies that might last an hour or two, many churches also sponsor weekend retreats that are gender segregated. The themes and issues addressed are usually similar to those addressed in the context of the church, but the intense focus over the course of a weekend, in a setting removed from the demands and distractions of everyday life, adds intensity to the experience and to the resulting bonding among the participants.

Gendered Parachurch Ministries

One major source of gendered association available to men is involvement in Promise Keepers. Founded in 1990 by Bill McCartney, the University of Colorado football coach, Promise Keepers is the fastest-growing segment of the evangelical men's movement. As has been mentioned, Promise Keepers encourages evangelical men to meet regularly with small groups of other men to explore what it means to be men of God. The most visible form taken by the movement is the rallies it holds in sports stadiums throughout the United States. The rallies are for men only (with the exception of some support staff members who are female). The conviction that women should not be part of Promise Keepers events prompted a controversy at one rally that was held to teach pastors about ministering to men who are Promise Keepers. Female pastors, even female pastors of churches that promote Promise Keepers, were barred from attendance.

The gender ideology promoted by Promise Keepers is somewhat ambiguous, ranging from traditional patriarchy to what Mary Stewart Van Leeuwen has called "soft patriarchy."[4] Promise Keepers plays down its patriarchal message by couching it in positive terms, encouraging men to be better husbands and fathers. But a look at Promise Keepers' literature clearly demonstrates its undeniably patriarchal character.

> The first thing you do is sit down with your wife and say something like this: "Honey, I've made a terrible mistake. I've given you my role. I gave up leading this family, and I forced you to take my place. Now I must reclaim that role."
>
> Don't misunderstand what I'm saying here. I'm not suggesting that you *ask* for your role back, I'm urging you to *take it back.* If you simply ask for it, your wife's likely to say, "Look, for the last ten years, I've had to raise these kids, look after the house, and pay the bills. I've had to get a job and still keep up my duties in the home. I've had to do my job *and* yours. You think I'm just going to turn everything back over to you?"
>
> Your wife's concerns may be justified. Unfortunately, there can be no compromise here. If you're going to lead, you must lead. Be sensitive, treat the lady gently and lovingly. But *lead.*[5]

Evans does not say how a Promise Keeper is to "take back" that leadership role in a marriage in which the wife does not agree that that type of leadership is legitimate.

Promise Keepers has been criticized for the way in which it slides back and forth between notions of godly manliness and manly godliness. In other words, as it points to Jesus as the model of true manliness, it implies that men are more perfectly created in the image of God than are women. Rebecca Groothuis and Douglas Groothuis make this point:

Defining masculinity as though it were the same thing as godliness can lead to a devaluation of femininity. If Christian men are like Christ not simply because they are Christians, but also because they are men, then men are simply more Christlike than women.[6]

Even more important than the different emphases of the meetings and retreats is this fact that regular association and intimate sharing with particular church members create bonds that shape church life itself. The gender division created and perpetuated by associations like Promise Keepers reaches beyond participation in meetings and talk about becoming better husbands and fathers. As just one example, many Promise Keepers members are heavily involved in the multilevel marketing telecommunications company Excell.[7] At Excell training meetings, they talk informally about Promise Keepers, and it is apparent that the Promise Keepers network has become a business network for many of those involved. In a context that does not offer similar bonding experiences that are not gender segregated (with the exception of "family" or "couple" activities), the result is a significantly gender-segregated community.

Gendered Social Events

While there are also gendered social events for women, and Women's Aglow has maintained a steady presence in the subculture, none of the women's organizations has reached the stature or level of influence of Promise Keepers. Women seem to be more influenced by ongoing social obligations that are also often gender segregated. For example, women are expected to attend the numerous wedding showers and baby showers held for church members, which in some churches may be almost weekly events. In an effort to meet the needs for adult interaction for stay-at-home moms, churches have organized "mom's day out" events in which child care is provided and moms are free to socialize with one another.

The choice of many Christian parents to educate their children at home is a widespread trend that contributes to the gendered nature of this subculture. While it is true that fathers often participate in teaching home-schooled children, the bulk of the responsibility seems to fall on mothers, and this creates an additional shared interest among mothers. Furthermore, many home-schooling families (usually the children and the mothers) meet for group instruction from time to time. This serves the dual purpose of allowing parents to provide instruction by others in areas in which the parents lack competence (perhaps a musical instrument or a sport), as well as the opportunity for the home-schooled children to gain socialization skills.

Father-and-son baseball games and fishing or camping trips provide social opportunities for bonding among the men in the church, although these seem less frequent than the social activities available to (and required of) the women.

Less Subtle Social Pressures

These sorts of institutional arrangements contribute to the creation of a gendered community, but they do not have this as their specific goal. In fact, the hidden aspect of their influence is a significant source of their power to shape the culture and to remain immune from criticism. Other cultural norms, carry implicit judgments about appropriate behavior for men and women and bring subtle reproach to those who fail to, or refuse to, fit in.

One of my respondents, whom I'll call Deborah, now considers herself to be a mainline Christian. She told me about her church youth group for high schoolers and the gender socialization and expectations she encountered there. The youth group was pastored by a man who was a seminary graduate. His wife, who had no such training, sat in on the teachings. "There was an unwritten rule that, if after a meeting, the girls in the youth group had questions, they were to go to the pastor's wife with them." Deborah, a particularly curious and theologically minded young woman, always had several specific theological questions about what had been taught. After the service was over, "I'd always go to the front and ask my questions directly to the pastor. I was the only girl who did so and it was always clear to me that I was breaking the rules," she said.

Rebecca told me how she and her husband had worked together on a project that was to bring several local churches together in a united effort. After the couple had spent months working together and reporting to their pastor on the progress of the project, the pastor was still addressing all questions to Rebecca's husband. The pastor sometimes called the couple's home with questions, and if Rebecca answered the phone, he always asked to speak to her husband. Several times women reported that, when they expressed an interest in leadership in their churches, they were offered positions in the nursery or the Sunday school. Women who indicated that this was not exactly what they had in mind were reminded by church leaders that those who would lead in the church must do so by serving, with the clear implication that the women's motivations might be less than pure.

Jennifer broke the gender rules by choosing to keep her own last name when she married. Cindy, another woman in leadership in Jennifer's church, insisted upon calling her by her husband's last name, even though Jennifer asked her repeatedly not to do so. Cindy later told a researcher that Jennifer's husband's name was her "real" name and that she couldn't understand why Jennifer would not just accept that. While no serious repercussions befell Jennifer for her noncompliance, her status as an insider was always suspect because of her refusal to "go along."

We're All Family Here

The evangelical image of the family is a model for the structure of institutions and organizations. The notion of a hierarchy of command is one dimension of this, as is the view that people are responsible to and for one another in a way that transcends simple interest in supporting the institution or organization. This view legitimizes, to some extent, the involvement of colleagues and others in the personal lives of those with whom they work. While an employer's interest in whether or not an employee's spouse would be willing to relocate seems inappropriate in our larger culture, it is not unusual within the cultural expectations of evangelicals.

In many ways, however, the evangelical subculture fits psychological profiles of dysfunctional and abusive families. This observation was first pointed out to me by Diana Garland, the fired dean of the School of Social Work at Southern Seminary. As I thought about her comparison and how it fit with the material I had gathered in my other interviews, it was disturbing how clear the parallels were. The abuser (the person in power) rules through terror, and everyone around tries not to make waves and to hide the reality of the dysfunction from those outside. Like the family of an alcoholic that works together to hide the problem from outsiders, many of my interview subjects who were embroiled in controversy reported being pressured to keep their problems a matter of private disagreement between them and their institutions. Students who reported sexual improprieties indicated that their institutions tried to keep such reports from being made public and in the process failed to address adequately the concerns of the students. Southern Seminary's firing of Dean Garland was ultimately a result of her violation of a "gag rule" about the conflict over gender issues. As in an abusive family, this commitment to presenting an unblemished appearance to "the world," regardless of the cost, plays into the hands of those in power.

Another interesting parallel with dysfunctional families is the degree to which women who face these conflicts fight to stay within the subculture. Another woman I interviewed explained,

> We both (my husband and myself) bought into this "strong male, weak, passive, female." And because I was reared in the South . . . when I went to college my dad told me, they were paying for every bit of my education and I went to a prestigious school, that the goal of education was to get a husband. [He said,] "You are going to college to get a husband to take of you because I will no longer take care of you after you graduate; that will be your husband's job." And it turned out that I did not graduate with a husband, so what I did was join Campus Crusade's staff because I thought I was doing something right for God. . . . I'm going to go witness to the world and be a missionary and devote my life to God in this way. [This was just] another "big daddy" situation. It was very hierarchical and they could be daddy to me there. I was miserable, but I met my husband there; he was going to be my rescuer. I just jumped from one bad situation to another where this man was in total control of my life. And because we were both so convinced that that was what the Bible taught, I never questioned it. . . . But the only way I could survive in that marriage was to die emotionally.

While many do leave evangelicalism, many others do not. It is curious that some of these women live their entire lives striving to be accepted by a subculture that constantly minimizes their worth, their calling, and their participation. One woman in particular comes to mind as an example here. She had been in tension with the subculture for years for her feminism and her involvement in the "evangelical left" and was ostracized over what was believed about her sexual orientation. Yet she fought to be part of the subculture, refused to be called a liberal (a derisive epithet, second only to "feminist/women's libber" in this world). This case is an extreme one, but it illustrates a common theme. These women are harassed, ridiculed, belittled, ignored, and/or fired. Yet, many of them fight to retain a place in the subculture until they have been so completely abandoned by it that they must do otherwise.

Inventing (and Re-Inventing) the Past

The contestation of history is also an important dimension of the conflict over gender ideology. Both traditionalists and feminists insist that their position is most in accordance with "true" historic Christianity. Both sides have constructed a history in which their opponents are guilty of innovation and accommodation to secular culture. Piper and Grudem, referring to the activities of women in the history of the church, write:

> Women have done almost everything men have, and have done it just as well. The significant exception to that generalization is that, until the very recent past, the "office" of teaching and of the sacramental ministry, with the jurisdictional powers this implies, has been reserved for men. . . . In its broad central tradition and practice, the church—East and West and in a multiplicity of cultural and social settings—has consistently maintained that to men alone is it given to be pastors and sacramental ministers.[8]

Another traditionalist writes:

> This basic New Testament teaching has been held with a clear consistency throughout most of Christian history. Today, many Christians no longer accept the headship of the husband in the family, or even the idea of any role difference at all. . . . One cannot find even a small controversy in early tradition over who should be the head of the family, much less over whether there should *be* a head. Few areas in early Christian teaching are as uniform, and fewer still were held with the same consistency as long as this one, since the first Christian voices advocating a different approach were raised only in about the nineteenth century.[9]

The authors assert the novelty of feminists' ideas about women's roles with the underlying assumption that this, in and of itself, shows them to be false. They never acknowledge that at one time, orthodox Christology, the concept of the Trinity, and even Protestantism itself were also new.

Evangelical feminists point out that, given the cultural context and the pervasive attitudes toward women, any example of a woman being treated as equal to men is more than a minor oddity to be ignored. They have written extensively about examples of equality and women's leadership in the Old and New Testaments and in the history of the church. Many professionally trained historians who come out of evangelicalism have chosen to write on this topic because of its personal importance to them.[10]

The historians Janette Hassey and Margaret Lamberts Bendroth have argued that antifeminism did not become the dominant perspective in Protestant fundamentalism until well into the 1920s.[11] Both present evidence of early fundamentalist support for women's ordination, women's public preaching, and women's active involvement in ministry leadership. Hassey writes: "At the turn of the century, Moody [Bible Institute] women openly served as pastors, evangelists, pulpit supply preachers and even in the ordained ministry."[12] She draws on documentary evidence from Moody Bible Institute to show its support for these women leaders. Women were granted pastors' degrees as late as 1929. Hassey tells of women who preached with the likes of R. A. Torrey and Billy Sunday. She also notes many of the earliest contributions to what has become the biblical feminist literature including Bushnell's *God's Word to Women,* and Jessie Penn-Lewis's *Magna Charta of Women* both written in 1919.[13] Incidentally, Hassey establishes Lewis's credentials as a fundamentalist, in part, by citing Lewis's authorship of an article on Satan for the *Fundamentals.*[14]

Bendroth goes to great lengths to explain the apparent discrepancy between the antifeminist public rhetoric of early fundamentalists (as demonstrated by DeBerg) and the fluidity of the actual practice of gender role limitations. She argues that when fundamentalists needed the efforts of women for aggressive evangelization, women were encouraged to take leadership roles. But, by the late 1940s and 1950s, the larger culture was urging women back into the home, and fundamentalism followed suit, limiting leadership roles for women. This move toward limiting women's roles was not a fundamentalist reaction in opposition to the larger culture but a development in accordance with, and taken as part of, that larger culture.[15]

Despite cries of *sola scriptura* (the Reformation call for basing beliefs on Scripture alone), tradition carries tremendous weight in the evangelical subculture. That which is believed to be oldest is always considered most authentic, unless a strong argument can be made for rejecting it. The "old-time religion" is thought to be concretely similar to that practiced in the time of Jesus. But, while many scholars have accepted this characterization, others have not. Martin Riesebrodt, for example, has argued that in "traditionalist" movements, efforts to make the tradition relevant inevitably result in rearrangement, addition, and innovation.[16]

Both traditionalists and feminists in the evangelical subculture attempt to legitimize their viewpoints by pointing to their own idealized versions of the past (i.e., the past in which their view held sway) and arguing that the "real meaning" of Christianity has been distorted by the other side. The contestedness of the history is very much a part of the current contestedness of gender ideology, and neither side in a debate such as this should be put forth as the "true" representative of the religious tradition. Both sides are grounded in dimensions of the history of the tradition, both sides represent innovations that are products of the late twentieth century, and both sides accuse their opponents of accommodating to and assimilating the demands of modern culture.

Living in a Material World: Gendered Evangelical Material Culture

Despite the categories created by scholars, people don't necessarily distinguish the sacred from the secular. As the historian Colleen McDannell has argued, "If we look at what people *do* rather than what they *think,* we cannot help but notice the continual scrambling of the sacred and the profane."[17] Indeed, within conservative Christianity we can find this "scrambling," even in what people think; the idea that God pertains only to certain dimensions of privatized life is considered terribly mistaken. Evangelicals believe God speaks to His people in the details of everyday life. They believe the Bible gives them guidelines, set out by God, for behavior in every dimension of life. Those outside this culture often voice skepticism at evangelicals who believe that there are "godly" positions on political issues, for example. But, within these communities there are books on how to manage your finances in a "godly" way; there are thought to be biblical requirements for just taxation; and the failure to get regular exercise is considered to be sinful.

McDannell examines religious artifacts, such as devotional pictures, crosses, and even parlor organs, and call them "tools" with which Christians "acknowledge common commitments, delineate differences, express affection, or socialize children."[18] She argues that religious objects can also be used as part of a purely "fashion aesthetic that has no connection to Christianity" to "communicate the taste and status of the family, irrespective of personal beliefs and commitments."[19] Indeed, as we shall see, many evangelical families create retro-Victorian homes that replicate and communicate the family's commitment to particular ways of ordering life based on nineteenth-century middle-class Victorian values: in both the nineteenth century and today, for example, the feminine style of decor demonstrates that the home is the woman's sphere. While it is true that "taste and status" can be separated from religion, it is also true that when evangelicals communicate "taste and status," those things in themselves are considered indicative of their beliefs and commitments. Seeking a home and family that reflect this Victorian ideal is a Christian duty. Women who excel in these skills are revered; women who don't fit the "Susie homemaker" role are somewhat suspect.

At times, people can use the material dimensions of religion to demonstrate their insiderhood, giving themselves room to differ from expectations on significant points.[20] Modeling this gendered Victorian ideal often also gives conservative Christian women latitude on other issues. The best example of this tactic is probably the well-known women political leaders in various religious right organizations who are dedicated to careers—careers that exist largely to promote the idea that it is best for women not to have careers.

In particular, in her discussion of "art" and "kitsch," McDannell helps us see clearly the ways in which ideas about gender have played into the devaluation of some forms of culture and the elevation of other forms.

> [Gender] is a symbolic system of social location that signifies established power relationships within a society. Masculine and feminine are contextually defined and repeatedly constructed. . . . I argue that these Christians were concerned with gender as much as aesthetics. To create a particular identity of "art" there must be a reference to some other that is non-art. The discussion of art and kitsch is also a discussion of where men and women, masculinity and femininity, fit into twentieth-century Christianity.[21]

When Christian culture makers wish to elevate one form of culture over another, they define the cultural form to be devalued as effeminate. Thus "art" is masculine and "kitsch" is feminine. Furthermore, in a distinction between textual culture and material culture, text is masculine and material is feminine. Culture makers seek to remasculinize Christianity by devaluing or eliminating cultural expressions they perceive as feminine and emphasizing those seen as masculine: text, doctrine, ideas.

But, in preferring the textual dimensions of religion over the material ones, scholars have traditionally also defined religion in terms that captured the dimensions controlled by elites (mostly men) and underplayed the dimensions that shape the living of religion by lay people (a majority of whom are women). Thus, we end up with definitions of evangelicalism that are rooted in theological disputes and pertain only indirectly to the tradition as it is experienced by believers. And if, as Barbara Wheeler has argued, "shaping and being shaped by the culture"[22] are what define membership in this group, the gendered nature of the culture evangelicals produce takes on significant importance. If the evangelically produced material culture is essentially gendered, then evangelicalism itself is essentially gendered. I contend that it is.[23]

The products marketed to conservative Christians can give us a sense of the way in which evangelical material culture reflects the American Protestant movement's gendered nature. While a few scholars have attended the Christian Booksellers' convention, one of the largest trade shows in the country, and marveled at the material culture exhibited there, one need only visit a local Christian bookstore to see examples firsthand.[24] Most communities of any size have these bookstores; the Santa Barbara community has two. Visiting these bookstores in several parts of the country, I was struck by their similarity (and by the minimal regional diversity). They market the accoutrements of a distinctive subculture.

The sentimentally sweet feeling of the bookstore is pervasive. Everyone is quite friendly and smiles and speaks in soft tones. Contemporary Christian worship music plays audibly throughout the store. And, while the tapes and compact discs are professionally produced versions of songs one might hear at an evangelical church service, they are intended for use by individual Christians at home or in the car. If you have spent any time around evangelicals and know the words to any of the songs, it's hard to keep from singing along.

Despite the fact that these are nominally bookstores, less than half of the inventory actually consists of books. In addition to things you might find in secular bookstores, such as cards, videos, and music tapes and compact discs, these stores also carry tee-shirts, sweatshirts, bumper stickers, jewelry, plaques, posters, and other artwork with which to decorate Christian homes with Bible verses. Home decorations, in a pseudo-Victorian style, such as throw blankets and specialty pillows, knick-knacks, dried flower wreaths, candles, and the like fill the shelves and display space.

These stores carry children's toys that have Bible themes and tee-shirts, sweatshirts, and hats with Bible verses or clever evangelistic sayings. "Christian" jewelry, especially rings and pendants, is popular, as is the line of decorative figurines called "Precious Moments." Looking at the inventory of a Christian bookstore with an eye toward reflecting on the gendered nature of the material culture, I first went to the toy section to look at the ways in which children are socialized into gendered roles. The best examples are action figures for boys and dolls for girls. Despite differences in size (and facial expressions), action figures and dolls are, of course, gendered versions of the same toy. Yet, the boys' "Holy Land Heroes" are promoted as protagonists in "true stories of strength and courage." One version concerns "Joshua and his defeat of the Canaanites, and another depicts "Ramses II defeated by the God of Moses." There is no pacifism here!

The dolls, which are marketed in pink boxes, look a lot like Barbie dolls but are labeled "Women of the Faith." Little girls can choose from the characters of Mary, Ruth, or Esther, although there are few discernible differences among the dolls and nothing to suggest the strength or courage of these women in the Bible.

One bookstore carried several decorative items for boys and girls, presumably to be hung on the walls of their bedrooms. The themes of the exhortations and meditations on them were consistent with the themes of the toys. The artwork for boys depicted sports and included such prayers as "Lord, may my goals and ambitions always honor your name," "Lord, for this I pray, may my life be a witness at home, at school or at play," and "Never let the fear of striking out keep you from swinging." These verses stressed themes of strength, independence, activity, and courage.

One poster for girls depicted a gymnast, and the verse on it read, "I can do all things through Christ who strengthens me." While at first glance this may seem to parallel the exhortations to boys, it is actually much more passive and dependent. And this example was the only one that came close to those sold for boys. The other posters and plaques meant for girls emphasized friendship and angels, neither of which ever appeared on items intended for boys.

Had the gendered polarity of the bookstore inventory been limited to the children's items, it would have been reasonable to observe that its socialization of boys and girls is consistent with that of the larger culture. The continued popularity of Barbie dolls, for example, among young girls in the larger culture, in spite of feminist gains in society, is often noted. But what is most interesting is that the distinct demarcation between genders is carried through from the toys to the items intended for adults. While there is an element of genderedness to gifts and books in the larger culture, it is not nearly so prominent as it is in the Christian bookstores. Compare the Christian bookstores with mainstream chains stores like Barnes and Noble, Borders, and even smaller specialty bookstores, for example. While the more mainstream bookstores carry some books that are likely to appeal primarily to men or primarily to women, the vast majority of the books are not specifically intended for members of either sex. In the Christian bookstore, there is almost no inventory that is not intended specifically either for men or for women. For example, there were two gift plaques intended for people with particular vocations: "For the Policeman" and "She's a Teacher." Wall decorations intended for men had pictures of lions or majestic depictions of nature. The vast majority of the decorations, however, were clearly for the home (the woman's sphere) and were exaggeratedly feminine. Often even childlike, the items displayed for women were done in soft colors and had pictures of flowers, homey scenes, small children and animals, and teddy bears.

The importance of gendered divisions was nowhere more clear than in the book sections of the stores. One store had bookshelves labeled "best-sellers" and "new releases." Of approximately fifty books on these shelves, eleven were expressly geared toward either men or women, and the majority of these (seven) were written for/about men. An additional book dealt with Christians who are leaders in our culture. *Lambs among the Wolves: How Christians Are Influencing American Culture* contains sections on each of twenty-two well-known Christian leaders in various fields, describing who they are and what they have done. Nineteen of those included are men, while only three are women. And, even among the three women chosen, the examples given are women in "softer" fields, such as the entertainment industry.

Two of the four books written specifically for women were devotional books exalting female friendships. The third addressed the issue of healing the past, and the fourth was addressed to Christian women who have chosen to leave their careers in favor of staying home with their children. While there was one parallel book (on healing the past) written for men, the others had much more active, leadership-oriented subjects.

Moving from the presumably gender-neutral categories of best-sellers and new releases to the shelves of books on "women's issues" and "men's issues," the themes continue. The men's books are bound in rich colors and focus on themes of strength, courage, and leadership. Looking at the women's shelf, one first notices the radical difference in the color of the books; they blend together like a wall of soft pinks and blues. Among the books for women, there was not one book on courage or leadership. Instead, the books fell into one of three categories: devotional books, books on friendship, and books (many with clever, funny titles) about dealing with a chaotic home.

These same themes for men and women were emphasized in the other published materials available for sale. Pocket-size books for either moms or dads, calendars (both wall and desktop,) topical Bible companions, and so forth all emphasized leadership, courage, and duty for men and friends, family, and home for women.

There were shelves of "Christian fiction," which contained as many books as, if not more than, any other shelves in the store. In fact, a new Christian novel is produced every week.[25] Perusing this shelf, I observed that these novels were nearly all Christian versions of the popular romance novels. I asked the bookstore clerk who purchases them, and he told me that they are all bought by women and that they sell very well. There was nothing similar to a Tom Clancy novel, and the clerk told me that the only fiction books that are sold in any numbers to men are novels that offer fictionalized accounts of spiritual warfare and end-times conflicts.[26]

Finally, there are gender-specific versions of the Bible. There is a growing market for niche Bibles, including study Bibles with notes geared toward specific groups of people.[27] There is a Bible for seniors, a Bible for people in recovery, and, of course, a Women's Study Bible and a Men's Study Bible.

A Return to the Cultural-Production Model

The examples in the previous section illustrate the subtle use of social pressure to bring about compliance with gendered cultural rules, rules that not only reflect gendered dualism but also create situations that foster and perpetuate that dualism. Insofar as they become a taken-for-granted reality that both shapes and is shaped by individual selves, these behavioral codes become "the cues and markers that help us think of ourselves as bounded units of reality."[28]

According to the production-of-culture model, identity, including gender identity, is the product of a process that is both individual and communal, both public and private. The examination of subtle arrangements and little things is important as part of what Wuthnow points to as a recognition of

> the dependence of self-constructs on markers in the culture at large: the self is understood not only in terms of internal development but also as a product of external reinforcement.[29]

I suggest that one way in which conservative Christians have responded to the loss of a sense of place that has come with modernity is by grounding sacred symbols not only in sacralized geographical spaces but in the human body itself—the gendered human body. First, like sacred space, the gendered body is ritualized in myriad ways. It enacts myths of masculinity and femininity and marks boundaries between the saved and the lost with idealized gendered behavior; in addition, ritual purity or defilement is the result of gendered behavior. Like sacred space, the gendered body is ritual space, "a location for formalized, repeatable symbolic performances."[30] When nearly all of life is ordered by gendered requirements, life itself becomes the performance of ritual in the space of the human body. Ritual often marks off the real world from "the way things should be." Thus, people can give assent to a traditionalist gender ideology and model it in certain dimensions of their lives, while at the same time living in ways that undermine the worldview they believe they support (e.g., Phyllis Schlafley, a woman who is a political activist, advocates that women mostly stay at home).

The gendered body "focuses questions about what it means to be human in a meaningful world."[31] For traditionalists, meaning comes for women via their gendered roles of wife and mother and for men via their gendered roles of leader and provider. Everyday activities become meaningful when they are seen as part of a cosmic plan. By fulfilling appropriate roles in a gendered dualism, men and women mirror the cosmic reality of the relationship between Christ and the church, God and the creation. For feminists, meaning comes from the expression of the self, possible only when one is freed from the constraints of socially constructed gender. For them, dimensions of masculinity and femininity are validated as they are both seen as integral parts of the nature of God.

The gendered body is clearly contested space. The ownership of sacred symbols of family and home is at stake in conflicts over the roles of women and men.

Sacred places are arenas in which power relations can be reinforced. . . . Sacred places are always highly charged sites for contested negotiations over the ownership of the symbolic capital . . . that signifies power relations.[32]

Those who violate gendered requirements subvert the power of the status quo. Indeed, they may do so as part of a strategy of desecration for the purpose of establishing their own right to control sacred symbols and to order reality according to their own interests.[33] The fact that the traditionalist Protestant sacralization of home and family is dependent upon a clearly delineated gender system is illustrated by conservative Protestants' opposition to gays and lesbians, who are seen as guilty of the most egregious violations of the gender dualism.

At the same time, though, as evangelical feminists criticize the patriarchalism, they also participate in its replication. They do so in overt ways: shoring up conservative Christian heterosexism, for example. They also, inevitably, do so in more subtle ways: essentializing the nature of women and viewing themselves in masculinist terms as the "Other."

Behavior, according to the production-of-culture model, is an important dimension of culture. Wuthnow criticizes those who would define culture as "non-behavior—mood, attitude, feeling—[that which is] only a perception or interpretation of the way reality actually is," claiming that they overly subjectivize the study of culture.[34] Emphasizing behavioral expectations, and especially the way in which they order, and are ordered by, other dimensions of culture, draws our attention to the reality that gender becomes gender in its performance.

6

What Do We Now Know about Conservative Protestant Women?

In addition to gaining a clearer picture of gender in the conservative Christian world, our focus on gender conflict and on the women who experience it also teaches us about those women themselves. This chapter explores the strategies and characteristics deployed by women to avoid and manage conflict, the ways in which these women actively participate in the construction of the gender ideology with which they live, and some of the specific responses of the women caught in conflict.

Strategies for Managing Conflict

As we shall see, the strategies used by women who most often avoid or survive conflict are, in a sense, all grounded in an attempt to minimize the significance of the challenge posed by their leadership. Women who create the perception that their presence as leaders would not challenge any other aspects of the cultural system face much less difficulty than women who, either intentionally or inadvertently, are controversial on other points as well.

My respondent Laura is not alone in exhibiting a courageous willingness to deal with the pain and rejection of being a woman pastor in order to be true to what she believes God has called her to do. As students in seminary, women are often told by spouses, relatives, friends, fellow students, and professors that they are mistaken about what they believe to be their callings. Facing opposition and discouragement at every turn, Laura still felt certain about God's calling:

Since I was eight years old I aspired to be a minister. My dreams were never opposed until I became a "Christian" at age sixteen, and we became involved in a conservative church. I was dissuaded strongly by everyone in that church network, later by college professors and students at Christian college.

Another woman told me,

I became a pastor because I was so clearly—unmistakably!—led to it by the Lord that I simply could not do otherwise. It was another step in a lifetime of following the Lord's leading and was a surprise—and a joy—to me!

I asked these women about their sources of strength and their networks of support and found the same answers over and over. Those successful in congregational ministry always cited the members of their own congregations as essential support networks. In one situation, a woman who later became a pastor was working as the Sunday school superintendent (and teaching Bible to men) in a church when a new pastor who opposed women in such roles was hired. The tension between them eventually led him to attempt to strip the position she held of any authority. When this failed, he brought her before the board on charges of insubordination (for refusing to give up her activities as superintendent) and heresy (for teaching men and teaching that women are permitted to teach men). He recommended that she be asked to leave the church. The male leaders in the church backed her and eventually asked the male pastor to leave. One of the women in parachurch ministry found that her local church was her base of emotional support and encouragement: "My local church is team-led by men and women and I am extremely supported there."

Women in these positions also cited the importance of networks of other women in Christian leadership and the supportive materials produced by evangelical feminist groups. The women I interviewed were all active in evangelical feminist organizations, and these associations were clearly central to them, although I cannot claim that this is the case for all women pastors. As one of my respondents put it,

In my early twenties I faced a lot of opposition from friends and leaders because I expressed my desire to go into the ministry full time. Those were difficult, turbulent years until I finally began to gain an understanding of redemption and who I am in Christ. Then I discovered more and more egalitarian literature and my footing became even stronger. I think, during this time, my greatest challenge [was] to be bombarded with teaching that stressed the submission of women in the church and the home, and having no one to share my concerns with.

In order to connect with those who share their concerns, these women ministers attended conferences sponsored by evangelical feminist organizations, stayed in touch with each other through newspapers and journals, and developed close friendships with other women ministers when they lived in a community large enough to have several; when they lived in more isolated areas, they managed to develop friendships across significant distances.

The women who remained married almost always indicated that their husbands were their most important supporters: "My husband is happy to serve in a supportive role at the church as needed. Weekly he prepares the coffee and sets out the snacks for us to enjoy at the close of the worship service—his favorite job!" Another woman said: "Whenever I have been challenged in my position it is always very hard for me to deal with it. But my husband always supports me and helps me get my perspective back. He also is the first one to stand up for me." The presence of a supportive husband and at least the appearance of a strong marriage contributed greatly to women's ability to avoid or survive conflict. In addition to providing moral support, husbands also made women leaders appear more "safe"; insofar as these women took on roles thought traditionally to be reserved for men, they were often considered a threat to "the traditional family" and even "accused" of being "pro-abortion, feminist, lesbians." By maintaining a strong family life centered around a traditional heterosexual marriage, these women thwarted such criticism.

Other women cited scattered examples of denominational support that they believed was crucial, such as a superintendent who urged women into leadership and who smoothed the way for them and denominational opportunities to speak and serve on important committees. The women seemed to agree that it was easier to be a woman pastor today than in past years:

I think it is easier to be a woman pastor now, because there is so much more support out there. . . . There are more prominent pastors that are female. There are workshops, even in our circles, that sincerely address female pastors. Stubborn arguing against female leadership is beginning to look silly in the face of many fruitful ministries led by women. There is also more literature available.

At the same time, these women were not unaware of recent trends that have been labeled a "backlash" against the gains women have made.[1]

One woman who pastored mainly in the context of an urban ministry believed that people in the city were more open to women in leadership than people in suburban and rural communities. She argued that urban ministry structures were less formal, permitting women more latitude, and she cited her colleagues in urban ministry as her most important and consistent supporters. This seems to parallel the experience of women on the mission field. Historically, even the most conservative fundamentalists and evangelicals have permitted women to preach to the "unsaved" in foreign lands. Limitations on women's preaching have almost always centered on women preaching to white, middle-class, American men.[2]

Early on, many women found individual mentors (some men and some women) who they believe made a tremendous difference in their success. Some of these mentors were pastors or evangelists; others were teachers in Sunday school, college, or even seminary; still others were colleagues the women met early in their careers. These mentors were able to help in several ways. First, by virtue of their own experiences, they were often able to point out pitfalls that the less experienced women had not seen. Second, mentors were able to assist with networking and lent credibility to the younger women. They could provide "endorsement," therefore making the women seem less controversial. Third, when conflicts did arise, mentors were often able to smooth them over and/or help the younger women to navigate through them.

Those women who could focus their efforts on a local congregation rather than a large institution seemed to fare better. Many women admitted that they made conscious efforts to avoid doing small things that might be threatening to men, trying to be "acceptable" and "pleasant." Some said that their more "relational" feminine style helped to mitigate tension. They avoided the label "women's libbers" or, worse yet, "feminist." Most repeatedly emphasized that they were not out to change gender boundaries but sought merely to do what God had called them to do. This was especially true of the more senior women.

Some of these women have chosen to work for broad-based evangelical acceptance of women's equality and thus have placed themselves in the midst of conflict. Others have self-consciously tried to avoid conflict but have been drawn into it by circumstances. I asked all of my respondents to try to assess why some women manage to negotiate the minefield success-fully and others do not. Those who had the fewest problems agreed that it was a matter of style:

> They know I give 100 percent. They know I really care about the college and the students and I'm trying to do the job. And . . . I'm not unreason-able. I can be a team player—I think of my demeanor, I'm small and pe-tite; the way I carry myself, my voice; just physically I'm a nonthreatening person.

The most commonly cited tactic for diffusing tension was to approach sit-uations with humor. A younger woman who later received tenure said, "I always use humor to challenge them on issues; that may not be the strongest way to do it but certainly was effective given who I was and who they were." Using humor to diffuse tension is a two-edged sword in these cases, though. Women who had the ability to joke and to be "one of the boys" believed that that tactic helped them avoid some of the pitfalls that had troubled others. On the other hand, this strategy had its own limita-tions, as it seemed to play into the existing view that women need not be taken seriously. Women who had been socialized in more "masculine" pat-terns of behavior believed that that often gave them an edge, seeming to confirm speculation that some of the problems arose by virtue of the diff-erences in style between men and women. When the people I interviewed described the women who managed to avoid some of the most serious difficulty, those women often ended up sounding rather genderless. They were usually older, often single, very proficient in their fields and exceed-ingly professional. One woman, for example, said that she was very ath-letic and had been raised in a family of boys, where she "learned how to shout." There seems to be general agreement that it is more acceptable for men to be angry than it is for women, but it may also be the case that men and women have different ways of being angry and that men's ways are more acceptable.

It also seems to be the case that women who bring to their institutions something that is seen as valuable on its own are given a bit more latitude than some others. One well-known female scholar who taught at a very Calvinist institution explained it this way:

I really am a Calvinist—I latched on to Kuyperian thinking because it has such a great creation theology—I really do believe that all of life is religion. . . . So, in one way, I was one of their best ambassadors. . . . They would often say to me, okay, you're our best ambassador, you're one of our best contacts with the evangelical Church at large.[3]

After knowing her as a Calvinist, these people then learned that she was also a feminist:

You could almost see the headache fumes coming up from their heads and saying, "And how are we supposed to put this together. We thought she was on our side. Now it turns out that she's a feminist!"

There also seems to be a group of more senior women who have been around a long time and have made it. Often they are highly respected by male faculty and students alike. There are two possible explanations for this. It might be that attitudes toward women have become more hostile in the past few years and that these older women would be facing more conflict if they were not now protected by tenure and seniority. On the other hand, it may be that they came of age in a time when they expected sexism. They may have learned to smooth things over with men by emphasizing their own timidity and deference. Younger women, on the other hand, expect to be treated as equals. Katy, a younger woman, told me about a more senior female colleague:

[She] probably has the record for being around here the longest. She can give you tales of discrimination. Like being left out of class senate hearings because they were talking about a man who had slept with a student. . . . She was asked not to show up and she wasn't given a reason. She never thought to ask for it. This was the mid-seventies and she never thought to ask for a reason because she thought it was as appropriate as they did.

Katy indicated that this woman had evolved into a feminist though she did not do so until after she was secure in her tenure.

Scholars have demonstrated that conflicts over women's ordination in the early nineteenth century differed in important and instructive ways from those of the late nineteenth and early twentieth centuries. At first, proponents of women serving in the pastorate did not undermine the prevailing gender ideology. Instead, they argued that some women had extraordinary calls from God, calls they should obey; that women's special roles related to their essential nature and required that they act to preserve the moral purity of society; or that there were pragmatic concerns that demanded that women pitch in. In other words, they argued that women should generally submit to their husbands and that generally men should lead the church but that, in certain cases, something unique about the woman's own God-given character or some special circumstance related to the state of the church made the case an exceptional one. But, by the late nineteenth and early twentieth centuries, those who supported the acceptance of female pastors were more likely to frame their arguments in terms of gender equality.[4] Scholars attribute this change to the growing presence of a movement for women's equality in the larger surrounding culture. I argue that this same dynamic is functioning on a smaller scale in the conservative Christian subculture today and that the different orientations toward women's roles are a function of generational differences. The older cohort of evangelical women who are serving as pastors do not defend their positions through claims of gender equality. They have been exposed to evangelical feminism, but they most often have learned of it as an alternative viewpoint, one that helped them make sense of what they already believed to be their calling from God. They defend their positions by playing down the degree to which they are controversial and by claiming that they serve in pastoral roles by the authority of God himself. The younger generation, on the other hand, is surrounded by the influence of feminism (evangelical and secular) and takes for granted many of the changes brought about by the older generation. They therefore see the issues facing them more clearly as issues of equality and are much more likely to frame them as such.[5]

Pamela and Victoria live somewhat on the edge of the professional ministry; they are barely tolerated by their colleagues and focus their attention on their own local congregations. They are both older (they became pastors late in life after their families were grown), and this seems to have shaped their responses to the conflicts they experience. Whereas the younger women I spoke with were more inclined to confront issues of sexism and even to take disputes to appropriate authorities, these older women most often let things slide and worked to find ways around the immediate problems without making too many waves.

Pamela admitted that she didn't rock the boat very often. Referring to whatever roadblocks she did encounter, she said, "I go around a lot—or I

rock the boat in gentle ways maybe that don't get a lot of direct confronta-
tion." She consciously dressed in a way that would blend in with the men's
style while still being acceptably feminine (though decidedly asexual.) She
tried hard to be "pleasant." She said her daughters-in-law teased her about
her unwillingness to be confrontational.

> They think I should be far more outspoken. Probably one of the reasons
> [I'm not], at this point in my life anyway, is that I'm fifty years old. You
> know, if I'm going to be a pastor, be in the system, I know I'm too old to
> do a lot of challenging because I will just get opted out of the system. So I
> can either choose to make a real stand and always be aggressive, and I
> know that it won't last very long. . . . I would rather do what I feel I'm
> called to do and try to change the system from the inside.

Pamela was acutely aware that she was unlikely to be called as the pastor of
another church. She knew that her position was something of an anomaly.

Victoria reported attending a pastoral installation ceremony at a church
where, she said, "the congregation knows us well, and accepts me, knowing full well the position I hold in my church. There is a great bond of
Christian love among us all." The church she visited did not allow women
to be pastors, so, she told me,

> When the time came in the ceremony where all the visiting pastors were
> asked to come up front and place their hands on the new minister for a
> blessing, I did not join the men who were going up toward the altar. I felt
> the host congregation knew me and knew I was there. If any of them had
> asked me to go along up front, I would have. Since they did not, I stayed
> in my seat, feeling that it was not my place to cause trouble in a church. I
> think I made the right decision.

Instead of dealing with these big and small affronts by drawing attention
to the problems, these women went to great lengths to demonstrate that,
while their role might be controversial, they themselves would not be the
source of any controversy. They made conscious efforts to smooth things
over with the men in the congregation. One pastor reported, for example,
that she included men in strategically visible positions in the church services. These women were emphatic that they were "not out to prove anything" and that their focus was always on their responsibility to God for

the mission He had given them and not the response others had to their work.

> I have confidence in my God who has clearly told me that I am where he wants me to be, doing what he designed me to do. Also I have nothing to prove—I'm not out to show the world what a woman can do. I seek no prominence.

The younger women pastors have a much stronger sense of wanting to change things. A woman in her thirties listed her reasons for becoming a pastor, one of which was her "desire to be an example to women and men of female leadership." Laura, another thirty-something woman in the same parachurch ministry as Paula, explained that, while it had been "a hell of a road for these last ten years," she had "made a conscious decision—despite the oppression—to be an agent of positive change not an embittered and angry woman."

> I was working with [the parachurch ministry] for approximately three years as ministry staff under the area leader. When he left, a white male was given the job to be my area leader. He was unequipped for the job. [So while] I functioned as AL as he learned his responsibilities over the first year. We then operated as an AL team but I had no title. I challenged the regional leader with the decision and clearly voiced that I felt I was the best qualified for the job. Local committee members recognized the decision as sexual discrimination but I chose not to vocalize their beliefs to the regional leader. I chose to stay believing that God had called me to this job and learned a tremendous amount from the oppression I faced.

Scholarly explanations of antifeminist fundamentalism and evangelicalism have tended to underplay the role of fundamentalist and evangelical women in the construction of gender identity. Yet there is simply too much evidence of women's active participation in the debate over gender to see contemporary American conservative Protestant gender ideology as merely constructed by men and imposed on women. Groups such as Concerned Women for America, Eagle Forum, American Life Lobby, and the March for Life are led by women; many articulate exponents of "traditional family values" are women; and it is women themselves who ultimately decide whether to live out this gender ideology.[6] Many antifeminist women argue that they found the business world unfulfilling and chose to make children and home a higher priority in their lives. When they did so, it was often a fundamentalist religious community and its antifeminist gender ideology that gave them encouragement and support. Moreover, it should be noted that this elevation of the family makes demands on fathers, as well. Like women, men are expected to find their central callings as family members, rather than as career persons. Promise Keepers, for example, an antifeminist organization that espouses patriarchal models of male headship in the family, calls men to repentance for putting their careers first while neglecting the needs of their wives and children.

Despite the insistence of many female pastors that they are not advocates for women's rights, all of these women are at the center of an ongoing cultural battle over what constitutes appropriate roles for women. They are both symbolic and active participants—whether by design or by accident—in the production of gender as an aspect of culture.

Who Stays and Who Leaves?

As we have seen, for women who do not feel empowered by submission, the tension created between their own desires and expectations and the limits placed on them by those in authority can have devastating results. Women in conservative Protestantism who face gender-related conflict over their leadership roles, which is ultimately gender-related conflict about their very identities, show remarkable perseverance within those subcultures; they stay despite tremendous turmoil. As we have seen, they develop strategies to manage or minimize the problems they face, seek out emotional and spiritual support to work through their own pain and frustration, and work to transform the beliefs and practices of the religious community of which they are a part. Despite efforts to manage conflict, many women do not succeed in doing so. That failure tends to push them along a continuum of potential responses until they find one that allows them to reconcile the dissonance in their own lives.

To many outside these traditions, it seems strange that women who are in such conflict with a major part of their religion don't just find religious homes more to their liking, and, of course, many do. We now examine the various responses of these women to the conflict they face. We begin by exploring why leaving is so difficult, then look at the various options taken by those who less successfully manage the conflict; we conclude by looking at those who decide to leave conservative Protestantism and at the various forms their leaving takes. Some women leave for other Christian denominations that are more open to women's leadership but whose beliefs are nonetheless still orthodox. Many, for example, become Episcopalian. Others leave orthodox Christianity for alternative forms of religious or spiritual expression; they seek woman-centered religious traditions such as wicca, goddess worship, and neopaganism or diffuse expressions of spirituality such as New-Age religion. Still others, discouraged by their experiences and cynical about religious organizations, become secular agnostics and atheists, more or less leaving religion altogether.

Particularly for women raised in conservative Protestantism, it is very difficult to leave. Conservative religion often rejects the distinction between the sacred and the profane made in other, more worldly, denominations. Evangelicals and fundamentalists express this impulse as "making every thought captive to Christ" or "bringing all of creation under the Lordship of Jesus." What this means in this instance is every aspect of these women's lives is wrapped up in their conservative Christian subculture. A break with this community means much more than just attending a different church on Sunday morning. It means breaking from one's family of origin; it may mean breaking childhood connections for women who attended Christian schools; it may well mean breaking college ties as well, since many of these women went to Christian colleges. Finally, as we have seen, it often means the dissolution of one's marriage. In fact, because so much of this world is organized around the view that secular (i.e., worldly) schools, workplaces, and relationships are at best secondary to "Christian" ones and at worst sinful rejection of this worldview requires that the women rethink almost every aspect of their lives up to that point. Furthermore, while these forces impact everyone in this conservative Christian world they perhaps affect these women most profoundly. These are women, after all, who have chosen to maximize the integration between their religion and what many on the outside consider secular aspects of life; they have, by choosing a career in "full-time Christian service," sought to bring every part of their lives in line with their sense of calling from God.

Other factors also contribute to the difficulty of choosing to leave the conservative Christian world. As much as these women strain at the limitations placed on them, it takes a long time for them to move from believing that the stress is created by their own disobedience to seeing the community and its gender ideology as the source of the stress. They can spend years second-guessing themselves, wondering whether they are just being rebellious, wondering whether their choices are really just self-indulgent sin, wondering whether continuing on their current path won't lead them literally straight to hell.

To those of us who are not part of this world, it seems that one could leave conservative Protestantism while remaining a "true" Christian, but this is not so for those in this world. For the most part, mainline denominations (or liberal denominations, as they are called) are seen as inauthentic representations of the Christian church. In fact, many who convert to conservative Protestantism do so from mainline denominations and don't consider themselves to have been Christians before their "conversion." Recall Laura, at the beginning of this chapter, who wanted be a minister before she was "a Christian." Finally, though mainline churches may be more open to women's leadership, there is evidence to the contrary as well.

For many conservative Protestant women, in short, choosing to leave the conservative Christian world is very difficult because they see no possible life outside this world. That this is the case is supported by my research. The women least likely to leave are the women who grew up in the tradition. Those who convert to it often remember their lives before conversion and can therefore imagine a life after; those who convert later in life seem more able to leave than those who convert in their youth.

The women I studied seemed to progress along a spectrum of strategies in response to the conflicts they faced. They began by questioning themselves; they accepted that they were suffering because of their own sinful natures and sought to submit more fully to what they believed God commanded. At this point, many sought out the support of women like themselves and men in positions of leadership who were sympathetic. As they did this, they encountered, often for the first time, biblical feminist interpretations of New Testament texts thought to restrict women. While I have argued throughout that culture is more significant to understanding conservative Protestantism than is theology, it is nevertheless hard to overestimate the impact of discovering that there might be other ways to read these texts that do not require women's subordination. Conservative Christians are convinced that their theology is based on "what the Bible says." In fact, many do not recognize the interpretation process at all, believing that the text says just what it says and that its meaning is so clear that all Christians who read it should understand it the same way. These women often indicate that they "know in their hearts" that God has called them to their work. Yet, until they find biblical feminism, they themselves struggle with the seeming contradiction between what they believe to be their calling and what they believe the Bible says. Learning that there are other possible readings frees them tremendously.

They most often encounter these alternative readings through organizations that are working to change the subculture's theology and to help women avoid and/or deal with gender-related conflict. Such groups include Christians for Biblical Equality, the Evangelical Women's Caucus, and the Center for Christian Women in Leadership. These women also found conservative Protestant institutions that already had different views on gender, including several of the conservative Protestant seminaries and various ministries and parachurch organizations. As part of these groups, many of the women felt at home; with like-minded conservative Christians, many of them were able to remain part of the subculture and at the same time hold views different from the dominant ones. Particularly if they were adept at the negotiating strategies discussed previously, or if something about them made them highly valuable to the subculture (such as prestigious family ties), many of these women continued to function in leadership roles in conservative Protestantism. They often even came to a decision to stay and to try to bring about change and to help other women facing similar problems as part of what God had called them to do. Many of the women who stayed told me, in essence, "Although I might be happier elsewhere, I can do more good for others by staying, despite the difficulty."

Others, though, who were not able to avoid and/or manage conflict, either because they lacked the social skills to do so, because they found themselves in the most hostile of environments, because they had no other cultural capital with which to avoid conflict, or because they were ultimately committed to their view that the inequality was wrong, were unable to reduce the tension to a tolerable level. Many of these women continued to function within the conservative Christian community for a time but found themselves eventually facing a crisis that led to a decision to leave. In the cases I studied, some women were still so reluctant to decide to leave that they did so only after having been "chased out," so to speak; they had been denied tenure and had therefore lost their jobs, or they had been removed from their pastorates and were therefore similarly unemployed. The period of transition for them was traumatic, but, once their separation from the subculture was complete, many found that they were surprised by the extent of their newfound sense of freedom. Leaving had seemed impossible; yet, once they had left they often felt that their journey had been characterized by a degree of inevitability.

The women who choose to leave conservative Protestantism fall into three categories: those who go to other Christian denominations, those who find a home in alternative religions that are considered woman centered, and those who leave religion altogether and become more or less secular. While most mainline Christian denominations have much more egalitarian views than the conservative branches, they typically do not embrace these women's largely conservative theological views. Of the mainline denominations, Episcopalism seems a common choice for women leaving conservative Protestantism over gender-related issues. Episcopalians have a strong intellectual heritage balanced by an emphasis on mysticism and tradition, and in many ways they do not fit a liberal/conservative division. They seem to blend the two, being theologically pluralistic but liturgically often very conservative. There are even significant evangelical factions within this denomination, which is most often thought of as liberal and mainline.

However, many women do stay. Some reinterpret submission theology in ways that they see as empowering; others continue to struggle, hoping to transform the subculture. As we have seen, they stay because leaving is difficult, but they stay also because staying is meaningful to them in other ways. Conservative Christianity is appealing because it is successful at creating meaning, order, and purpose. In the conclusion, we look at the way gender ideology contributes to the creation of that meaning, order, and purpose.

Conclusion

> To understand the character of social conflict is to understand some-
> thing of the changing nature and constitution of the social order—
> the deepest ways in which civilizations are ordered and legitimated.
> The reason is that social change, more often than not, occurs in and
> through conflict.[1]

If religions and religious institutions produce and reproduce themselves
in the context of explicit conflict and subtle coercion, then the stories
of the women on the margins of legitimacy in those traditions should
provide rich data for examining the mechanisms by which they do so.
Yet, the process of teasing out these mechanisms is a difficult one, in
part because one of a subculture's most effective ways of reproducing
itself is to hide those mechanisms of production. In fact, the more
effective the process, the harder it is to find the mechanisms. When
people believe things are as they always have been (or that innovations
will move them further from some ideal time), that grave consequences
will result from ordering society in any manner different from the current one, or that anyone who does not support the status quo is either
evil or deranged or is making a fuss about nothing, challenges to existing authority can be rendered powerless. It is instructive that those
who would challenge the gender structure of conservative Protestantism
are portrayed by its defenders as both terribly menacing (rebels who
would "destroy the family") and tediously irrelevant ("libbers" who
make a fuss out of things that are no big deal), leading an observer to

conclude that someone is invested in silencing the critics of the gender structure.

Women, Fundamentalism, and Ethnography

The growing interest in women and religion and the rise in popularity of ethnography as a research method are inextricably tied to each other. Since the experiences of women are often neglected in documentary and textual sources, ethnography is a key tool for those who would examine religious cultures with an eye toward gender inclusivity. This is especially true with regard to sociological and historical studies of women in conservative religious traditions, because such women are even less likely to have a voice in the formal structures of religion.

As feminist scholars moved from an emphasis on the patriarchal character of conservative religion and began to grapple with questions about why women seem, at times, to be at home in such traditions, they resorted to a variety of explanations that rarely took seriously what the women said about their own lives. Women in conservative religion were seen as misguided dupes or as disingenuous manipulators who benefited personally from the oppression of their sisters.

Postmodern critical reflection led scholars in many fields to recognize that scholarship, by its very nature, tends to assemble vast amounts of data into singular narratives and thereby silences counterhegemonic voices. In the study of religion, one finds a new emphasis on the exploration of the various aspects of complex phenomena, much criticism of scholarship that imposes univocality on social systems as though they were monolithic, and many calls to explore conflict and contestedness as essential components of cultural production.[2] Furthermore, postmodernism has challenged us to take seriously the "insider-outsider problem" and to be more cognizant of the ways in which our work is shaped by our own values and perceptions.[3]

Ethnography, as a method, is held up by many as a potential answer to these longstanding criticisms; "ethnographers can give voice to the otherwise voiceless," or so the story goes. And so it should come as no surprise that the many fine recent studies of women and religion have, at the very least, significant ethnographic components.[4] These ethnographies represent a move away from a feminist critique of traditional religion and toward an effort to make sense of the women in these traditions on their own terms; yet, each falls short in terms of taking into consideration the conflict over gender and the implications of that conflict for the shaping of conservative religious culture.

Collision of Symbolic Worlds

Creative blending notwithstanding, traditionalist and feminist ways of understanding and ordering reality are profoundly different; in each, the gendered human body becomes the symbolic representation of that ordering. In the context of conservative American Christianity, battle lines are often drawn between those who see reality as grounded in a fixed, gendered dualism and those who see gender as a blending of biology and fluid, amorphous, socially constructed categories. When representatives of each view vie for control of the tools of cultural production and reproduction (be they religious institutions, ideological perspectives, or any other aspect of, or holding place for, cultural capital), tremendous conflict ensues. This is not to argue that everyone is part of the battle; many people are not. The point is that, in evangelicalism's internecine battles, gender is often an important dimension of the conflict and often the dividing line itself.

As sources of tremendous power in the production of culture, institutions are also often sites of conflict. Two types of institutions play important roles in the production of culture. First, there are those institutions that exist for the purpose of ensuring the continuation of the subculture itself, institutions that give shape and definition to the future of the subculture and that are themselves tools for the production of culture over which combatants battle. Second, there are institutions that are themselves combatants. Such institutions exist to promote the adoption of one perspective over another, of one set of norms over another, of one worldview over another.

In many instances, culture producers in the evangelical world have made gender the all-important issue. Conflict over gender issues has destroyed individual lives and brought institutions to the brink of disaster. Evangelical leaders have chosen gender issues as a litmus test of orthodoxy when they could have more easily found support in their own history for at least tolerating a diversity of opinions. They have rationalized rudeness as an appropriate response to perceived lack of obedience to biblical command, and they have placed debatable interpretations of biblical restrictions on women's roles above much clearer biblical commandments to love one another.

Tensions over these issues clearly run much deeper than is reasonable for decisions over, for example, who is to have the title "pastor." Such tensions point to bigger issues that are symbolized by the conflicts over the roles of men and women. This seeming obsession of conservative Protestants with issues related to gender has been explained variously. Randall Balmer has identified beleaguered fundamentalists with the endangered fetus in the abortion debate.[5] According to Balmer, fundamentalist men seek to limit the public lives of women in order to retain the childlike security found in the all-sacrificing, apotheosized mother. Karen McCarthy Brown argues that, realizing they could control very little of the outside world, fundamentalist men opted to control "the other" within: women.[6]

Karen Torjesen teaches courses on women and religion at Claremont Graduate School and is herself a former evangelical who faced what she considered to be gender-related problems in her career. She proposes that part of the reason evangelical men have difficulties dealing with evangelical women who are not subordinate is a "fear that women can't be controlled." She says:

> I think it has to do with the construction of "the other". . . . When you know someone shares a common culture with you, you are confident that you know what their values are, what kinds of commitments they have, what kinds of decisions they'll make. . . . When women are "the other" . . . it is as though she comes from another culture and therefore she is frightening because she is not predictable.[7]

A significant part of the appeal of evangelicalism is that it is an ordered system that provides clear answers to life's questions. This is clearly of value to those who embrace this form of Christianity, and it should not surprise us that the need for order (and control) plays a role in the gender ideology. But, ultimately, I think the matter goes even deeper than this. Conservative Protestantism is grounded in an extremely dualistic ideology that emphasizes the gulf between the Creator and the creation. The creation itself is further divided into good and evil, light and darkness, saved and lost.

For the conservative traditionalists, masculinity and femininity symbolically represent these cosmological polar opposites. Male and female are the earthly embodiment of the cosmological dualism. Sharp delineation between them replicates the order of the cosmos, and blurring the distinctions between them threatens the order itself. People who cannot, or will not, live within their assigned spheres challenge not only the gender norms but the symbolic reality and the order it represents, as well. Those unwilling to conform to "God's order" and its gendered requirements are the fullest representation of the arrogance of humanity in late modernity: rebelling against God, they seek to be autonomous individuals, "creating themselves" in a Nietzschean sense in place of accepting their role as the crowning glory of God's creation. They symbolize a disorder and chaos that threatens to destroy the meaning, order, and purpose that are to be found only in living according to the Creator's plan.

While masculinity and femininity symbolize the boundary between cosmic polarities, identification with traditionalism, on the one hand and feminism on the other mark the two positions located on either side of a dividing line or boundary that separates earthly ideologies. Some traditionalists articulate a more stringent traditionalism than they practice, often because it is a way of drawing a line between themselves and the rest of culture, including their evangelical cousins, whom they see as a bit too "worldly." Other traditionalists who wish to minimize the social distance between themselves and the rest of the culture (often for purposes of evangelism) articulate support for women's equality but, in practice, do little to bring it about. Feminists, on the other hand, wear their support for women's equality as a badge to demonstrate that, while they are evangelical, they are not like "those evangelicals who are really fundamentalists" and that, while they are feminists, they are not like "those feminists" who are anti-Christian and antifamily.

So, in fighting over the power to decide what evangelical gender ideology will look like, the combatants are actually fighting over the power to define the whole subculture—to produce a subculture that is in line with their own ways of looking at the world and that preserves their interests.

Scholars have only recently begun to take seriously the significance of gender and gender-related issues for understanding American Protestant fundamentalism. This is increasingly important as conservative Christianity continues to exercise influence on American culture and politics. While the public focus on the abortion issue may be waning, battles over gay and lesbian rights seem to be on the rise. However, we must understand that, contrary to popular belief, fundamentalists are not monolithically rigid in their views about appropriate gender roles. The simple view that gender norms are created by men and imposed on women is increasingly seen as inadequate. I have argued for the view that conservative Protestant attitudes and behaviors with regard to gender are (and have been historically) characterized by fluidity, rather than rigidity. We cannot posit a "pure fundamentalist" perspective on gender rooted in the past and then consider departures from it to be accommodation to the larger culture. On the contrary, both feminist and antifeminist perspectives are part of the complex and often paradoxical American Protestant fundamentalist tradition. Cultural norms and expectations concerning gender, within this subculture, are part of a larger process of cultural production. Profeminist perspectives and practices are, indeed, developed in interaction with the larger culture. Such factors as fundamentalists' need for manpower (so to speak) for evangelization, the ability of women who do not work outside the home to contribute time to fundamentalist social concerns, the need for two incomes to support the much-lauded family, and the impact of the larger feminist movement have all played parts in the development of biblical feminism.

Antifeminist perspectives and practices have also been shaped in the context of the larger society. The reaction of fundamentalists to their perceived loss of power in American culture, fear over the changing roles of women, the "feminization" of American religion, social problems that are exacerbated by the breakdown of the nuclear family, and women who choose homemaking over careers outside the home are examples of the developments to which antifeminist fundamentalists have responded.

While production of culture models bring into focus important dimensions of the relationship between religion and culture—and religion as culture—sociological models that highlight the production of culture without a focus on conflict miss as much as they illuminate. Culture is both explicitly and implicitly produced. It is produced by elites in the ideologies they create and articulate and the institutions they control; culture is also produced by nonelites through a process that entails molding of the elite's proclamations into frameworks for everyday life. Seemingly sanitized categories like the allocation of resources and the analysis of discourse have the potential of obscuring the important role of ongoing conflict in the production of culture. The war stories we have explored elucidate an important aspect of that production.

Having gathered the war stories, made the case for their importance to understanding conservative Christianity, and made some preliminary observations as to how they play out in the production of the subculture, we find that many questions still remain. We need to find better ways to construct multilayered narratives that can weave the variety of voices together to better represent the complex world in which we all live. We need to better understand the hidden ways in which culture, values, mores, and ideology are produced and reproduced. And we need to better understand whose interests are served by those processes of production and reproduction.

Finally, it is my hope that this focus on the war stories has served two purposes: to add another chorus of voices to the scholarly portrayal of conservative Christian women and to call our attention once again to the complexity of this subculture.

Notes

NOTES TO INTRODUCTION

1. Joy Charlton, "What It Means to Go First: Clergywomen on the Pioneer Generation," paper presented at the annual meeting of the Society for the Scientific Study of Religion, St. Louis, Missouri, October 1995.

2. R. Marie Griffith, *God's Daughters: Evangelical Women and the Power of Submission* (Berkeley: University of California Press, 1997).

3. Ibid., 172.

4. Ibid., 147.

5. Ibid., 150.

6. Ibid., 155.

7. Ibid., 95.

8. Ibid., 120.

9. Ibid., 152–156.

10. For examples of this literature see Letha Dawson Scanzoni and Nancy A. Hardesty, *All We're Meant to Be: Biblical Feminism for Today* (Grand Rapids, Mich.: William B. Eerdmans, 1992); Rebecca Merrill Groothuis, *Women Caught in the Conflict* (Grand Rapids, Mich.: Baker Book House, 1994); Virginia Hearn, *Our Struggle to Serve* (Waco, Tex.: Word Books, 1979); Kari Torjesen Malcolm, *Women at the Crossroads* (Downers Grove, Ill.: InterVarsity Press, 1982).

11. Brenda Brasher, *Godly Women: Fundamentalism and Female Power* (New Brunswick: Rutgers University Press, 1998).

12. Ibid., 4.

13. Ibid., 6.

14. Ibid., 13.

15. Ibid., 69.

16. Ibid., 7.

17. Ibid., 41.

18. Ibid., 71.

19. Ibid., 88.

20. Ibid., 63.

21. Ibid., 72.

22. Ibid., 134.

23. See Colleen McDannell, *Material Christianity* (New Haven, Yale University Press, 1995), for a discussion of the ways in which elite biases for theology and "high religion" have silenced "women children and other illiterates" and, in the process, created a distorted image of religion.

24. I do not see it as appropriate to my role as researcher to challenge the status quo, but neither do I see it as my role to support it.

25. My bibliography contains a list of the published materials.

26. Ernest R. Sandeen was among the first scholars to depart from the reductionism of "status anxiety" definitions and to seek to understand the tradition in more complex terms. In *The Roots of Fundamentalism: British and American Millenarianism, 1800–1930* (Chicago: University of Chicago: 1970), Sandeen argues that fundamentalism was rooted in theological concerns: first, millenarianism and, second, reformed doctrines about the inerrancy of Scripture contained in the so-called Princeton Theology. In 1980, when George Marsden published his *Fundamentalism and American Culture: The Shaping of Twentieth-Century Evangelicalism, 1870–1925* (Oxford: Oxford University Press, 1980), he argued that the theological and intellectual roots of fundamentalism and evangelicalism were much broader than Sandeen had believed and that Sandeen had neglected the cultural context that shaped the movement.

27. For example, the author of the dispensationalist classic *The Late Great Planet Earth* (Grand Rapids, Mich.: Zondervan Publishing, 1970), Hal Lindsey, argues for his reading of the biblical text by claiming that he takes the Bible literally, while those who disagree with him do not. This before he goes on to explain that the locusts in the book of Revelation represent helicopters and that one of the nations referred to represents the Soviet Union. In fact, no one, even the most fundamentalist Christians, can take the Bible literally. This claim is merely a rhetorical move and is wholly inadequate as a definitional characteristic.

28. These definitional problems contribute to the difficulty in assessing the numbers of Evangelical Christians in America. According to George Gallup, some 31 percent of Americans can be counted as part of this group. George Gallup Jr. and Jim Castelli, *The People's Religion: American Faith in the 90s* (New York: Macmillan, 1989), cited in Wade Clark Roof, *A Generation of Seekers: The Spiritual Journeys of the Baby Boom Generation* (San Francisco: HarperCollins, 1993) 276.

29. For a more detailed discussion on the origins of fundamentalism in America, see George Marsden, *Fundamentalism and American Culture* (Oxford: Oxford University Press, 1980). For an analysis of the role of gender issues in the rise of fundamentalism see Betty DeBerg, *Ungodly Women: Gender and the First Wave of American Fundamentalism* (Minneapolis: Fortress Press, 1990), and Margaret Lamberts Bendroth, *Fundamentalism and Gender, 1875 to the Present* (New Haven: Yale University Press, 1993).

30. For more on this, see George Marsden, *Reforming Fundamentalism* (Grand Rapids, Mich.: William B. Eerdmans, 1987).

31. Barbara Wheeler, "You Who Were Far Off: Religious Divisions and the Role of Religious Research," Douglass Lecture, presented to the Religious Research Association, St. Louis, Missouri, October 1995, 14.

32. Susan Harding, *The Book of Jerry Falwell* (Princeton: Princeton University Press, 2000).

33. Ibid., ix.

34. For example, twentieth-century "conservatives" had much in common with nineteenth-century "liberals," both of whom were seeking tremendous social and cultural change. "Liberals" in the former Soviet Union were advocates of free-market economics, while "conservatives" supported the policies of the communist state.

35. While biblical feminists often choose to call themselves feminists, other feminists believe that evangelical Christianity (or biblical Christianity) and feminism are mutually exclusive and that those who embrace this form of Christianity cannot rightly call themselves feminist. This is sometimes a result of confusion on the part of feminists between biblical feminists, who embrace complete equality for men and women, and other conservative Christians who claim to support gender equality while maintaining some form of patriarchy. At other times, it is the result of the feminist conviction that any form of orthodox Christianity is essentially patriarchal and inevitably antifeminist. I have chosen to accept their self-designation.

36. George Marsden has argued that, because of the diverse, often paradoxical, streams of influence that shape these traditions, generalizations about evangelical (and, by implication, fundamentalist) views on issues relating to culture and politics are hazardous. See George Marsden, "Preachers of Paradox: The Religious New Right in Historical Perspective," in *Religion and America: Spiritual Life in a Secular Age*, ed. Mary Douglas and Steven Tipton (Boston: Beacon Press, 1982), 151.

37. George Marsden, *Reforming Fundamentalism: Fuller Seminary and the New Evangelicalism* (Grand Rapids, Mich.: William B. Eerdmans, 1987).

38. Jackson Carroll and Penny Long Marler, "Culture Wars? Insights from Ethnographies of Two Protestant Seminaries," *Sociology of Religion* 56, no. 1 (spring 1995): 1–20.

39. For examples of this scholarly literature see Judith Stacey, *Brave New Families: Stories of Domestic Upheaval in Late Twentieth-Century America* (San Francisco: Basic Books, 1990), and Judith Stacey and Susan Elizabeth Gerard, "'We Are Not Doormats': The Influence of Feminism on Contemporary Evangelicals in the United States," in *Uncertain Terms: Negotiating Gender in American Culture*, ed. Faye Ginsberg and Anna Lowenhaupt Tsing (Boston: Beacon Press, 1990).

40. James Davison Hunter, *Culture Wars: The Struggle to Define America* (San Francisco: Basic Books, 1991).

41. John P. Bartkowski, "Debating Patriarchy Discursive Disputes over Spousal Authority among Evangelical Family Commentators," *Journal for the Scientific Study of Religion* 36 (1997): 393–410.

42. I have placed these words in quotes to call attention to the difficulty of choosing adequate terminology. In fact, within this tradition, the existence of advocates for women's equality vastly predates the existence of the term "feminism." Furthermore, while the view we call "traditional" may have been the dominant view, alternative views are also very "traditional"; they have been present in the subculture for a very long time. Allowing one side in the conflict to claim the label "traditional" buys it significant coin in this subculture. As is often the case, a rhetorical battle is fought over the very terminology of the debate. That said, I have elected to call each side by the name it chooses for itself, thus avoiding siding with one over the other.

43. Some of the interviews on which this section is based were conducted as part of the research for this project; others were conducted, also by me, as part of a larger project Religion in Los Angeles, funded by the Pew Charitable Trusts and overseen by Wade Clark Roof.

44. This is not to say that moderate traditionalists and the more liberal evangelical feminists have not been involved in these conflicts. In fact, many women report experiencing sexism at the hands of those who continuously articulate their commitment to women's equality. In some ways, this more insidious discrimination is more frustrating because, being more subtle, it is harder to fight. And the reason that the more liberal feminists are not directly engaged in debate by the traditionalists is that they have largely been written off as no longer evangelical, despite their often strong desire to remain within the evangelical camp.

45. Specifically Genesis 3:16; 1 Corinthians 11:2–16; 1 Corinthians 14:33–38; 1 Timothy 2:8–15; Ephesians 5:22–33; Colossians 3:18–19; 1 Peter 3:1–7.

46. John Piper and Wayne Grudem, *Recovering Biblical Manhood and Womanhood: A Response to Biblical Feminism* (Wheaton, Ill.: Crossway Books, 1991), 306–312.

47. And, as I found in other contexts, had I been able to interview his wife, I might have heard a different interpretation.

48. Scholars have been somewhat divided over the degree to which Promise Keepers can be called "antifeminist." For alternative arguments see John Bartkowski, "Breaking Walls, Raising Fences: Masculinity, Intimacy, and Accountability among the Promise Keepers," *Sociology of Religion* 61, no. 1:33–53, and Bartkowski, *Servants, Soldiers, and Godly Men: Melange Masculinity among the Promise Keepers* (forthcoming).

49. In 1996, Promise Keepers rallies around the country drew crowds of more than one million men, and the national organization itself had a budget in excess of $100 million, according to Randall Balmer, "Keep the Faith and Go the Dis-

tance," unpublished paper presented at the annual meeting of the American Academy of Religion, New Orleans, November 1996.

50. Discussions over these biblical texts appear over and over in this literature. The following is not taken from one specific source but is, rather, a summary and illustration of the form and content of biblical feminist argument. Representative works include Kari Torjesen Malcolm, *Women at the Crossroads* (Downers Grove, Ill.: InterVarsity Press, 1982); Katherine Bushnell, *God's Word to Women,* privately published, 1912, 1923 (Mossville, Ill.: God's Word to Women Publishers); Charles Trombley, *Who Said Women Can't Teach?* (South Plainfield, N.J.: Bridge, 1985); Mary Stewart Van Leeuwen, ed., *After Eden: Facing the Challenge of Gender Reconciliation* (Grand Rapids, Mich.: William B. Eerdmans, 1993).

51. Katherine Bushnell, *God's Word to Women.*

52. Paul K. Jewett, *MAN as Male and Female* (Grand Rapids, Mich.: William B. Eerdmans, 1975.)

53. The material that follows is drawn from the study Religion in Los Angeles, funded by the Pew Charitable Trusts. The interviews were conducted during 1993.

54. For more evidence of this "creative blending" see Stacey and Gerard, "'We Are Not Doormats,'" and Stacey, *Brave New Families,* 151.

55. John R. Rice, *Bobbed Hair, Bossy Wives, and Women Preachers* (Murfreesboro, Tenn.: Sword of the Lord Publishers, 1941).

56. Colleen McDannell, "Creating the Christian Home," in *American Sacred Space,* ed. David Chidester and Edward T. Linenthal (Bloomington: Indiana University Press, 1996), 210–211.

57. Lynn Davidman, *Tradition in a Rootless World: Women Turn to Orthodox Judaism* (Berkeley: University of California Press, 1991).

58. Harding, *Falwell,* 168.

59. Ibid., 168.

NOTES TO CHAPTER 1

1. For a brief history of evangelical feminism as a movement, see Margaret Lamberts Bendroth, *Fundamentalism and Gender, 1875 to the Present* (New Haven: Yale University Press, 1993), 118 ff.

2. In 1991, Christians for Biblical Equality commissioned a survey of its membership to be conducted by C. J. Olsen Marketing Research, Inc., in Minneapolis, Minnesota. The survey was made available to me by Catherine Kroeger during my field research and indicated that CBE's membership is 75 percent female, 69 percent married, and 95 percent white; 58 percent of its members hold graduate degrees of some sort.

3. The data for this chapter are drawn from several sources. I have made use of a collection of books, tapes, articles, newsletters, and other documents produced and/or distributed by CBE. I spent nearly a week with the CBE founder Catherine

Kroeger at her home in Cape Cod in February 1995 and attended the CBE conference held at Gordon College in Wenham, Mass. in the summer of 1995. Kroeger graciously gave me access to her private collection of biblical feminist materials as well as free run of the archives of CBE. During those two research trips, plus additional trips to Los Angeles and San Francisco in the spring of 1995 and trips to Massachusetts, Pennsylvania, and Kentucky during the summer of 1995, I conducted twelve formal interviews lasting from forty-five minutes to several hours, as well as innumerable informal interviews, that have informed my field notes. A research grant from the Society for the Scientific Study of Religion underwrote the cost of having these interview tapes transcribed.

4. Gretchen Gaebelein Hull, "Biblical Feminism," *Priscilla Papers* 5, no. 3 (summer 1991): 1.

5. For an example of this point, see Mary Stewart Van Leeuwen, ed., *After Eden: Facing the Challenge of Gender Reconciliation* (Grand Rapids, Mich.: William B. Eerdmans, 1993), 31–36.

6. Hull, "Biblical Feminism," 2.

7. Gretchen Gaebelein Hull, "Inclusive Language," lecture given at the CBE conference, Wenham, Massachusetts, Gordon College, July 1995.

8. Gordon was a well-known fundamentalist and one of the founders of the seminary where Kroeger later taught.

9. Katherine Bushnell, *God's Word to Women*.

10. *Update* 10, no. 3 (fall 1986): 5–6.

11. This concern was expressed to me repeatedly in interviews and appeared in the discussion of the Fresno conference published in *Update* 10, no. 3 (fall 1986).

12. Kaye Cook, interview by author, 9 February 1995, Wenham Mass., tape recording.

13. While its remaining ties with EWC are strained, CBE maintains very friendly ties with MWG. In fact, MWG and CBE exchange speakers internationally from time to time.

14. This respondent requested anonymity.

15. Patricia Litton, interview by author, 24 January 1995, Ventura, Calif., tape recording.

16. John Piper and Wayne Grudem, *Recovering Biblical Manhood and Womanhood* (Wheaton, Ill.: Crossway Books, 1991), xiii.

17. For examples of these works see Paul K. Jewett, *MAN as Male and Female* (Grand Rapids, Mich.: William B. Eerdmans, 1975); Jewett, *The Ordination of Women* (Grand Rapids, Mich.: William B. Eerdmans, 1980); Charles Trombley *Who Said Women Can't Teach?* (South Plainfield, N.J.: Bridge, 1985); and Shirley Stephens, *A New Testament View of Women* (Nashville: Broadman Press, 1980).

18. For an example of this argument see Rebecca Merrill Groothuis, *Women Caught in Conflict: The Culture War between Traditionalism and Feminism* (Grand Rapids, Mich.: Baker Book House, 1994), 152 ff.

19. Margaret Fell was a Quaker and the wife of George Fox. Her seventeenth-century essay "Women Speaking Justified" put forth many of the arguments against scriptural interpretations that would keep women silent in churches that are still used by evangelical feminists.

20. Kari Torjesen Malcolm, "The Golden Age for Women Preachers," *Priscilla Papers* 6, no. 4 (fall 1992): 12; Julie Ann Flora, "Nineteenth-Century Women Hymn Writers," *Priscilla Papers* 8, no. 1 (winter 1994): 8.

21. CBE Resource Ministry, September 1995 catalog (St. Paul, Minn.: Christians for Biblical Equality), 5.

22. Marie Wiebe, interview by author, 23 January 1995, Camarillo Calif., tape recording.

23. Craig S. Keener, "Sexual Infidelity as Exploitation," *Priscilla Papers* 7, no. 4 (fall 1993): 15.

24. This statement appears in every issue of the *The Priscilla Papers* and every issue of *Mutuality*. Both are available from CBE.

25. Interview with Ginny Hearn, Berkeley, California, March 11, 1995.

26. I have argued elsewhere that homosexuality has actually replaced abortion as the cornerstone of the political agenda of the Christian Right. "From Right to Life to Anti-Gay Rights: Shifting Traditional Family Values," paper presented at the annual meeting of the Society for the Scientific Study of Religion, Raleigh, North Carolina, November 1993.

27. See Piper and Grudem, *Recovering Biblical and Womanhood*. The charge is made repeatedly throughout this work.

28. Piper and Grudem, *Recovering Biblical Manhood and Womanhood*, 84.

29. Ibid., 376.

30. Jewett, *MAN as Male and Female*.

31. Piper and Grudem, *Recovering Biblical Manhood and Womanhood*, 492.

32. Although I've cited names where possible, for obvious reasons many of these stories have been included without names.

33. These interviews were conducted between January and June 1995. While some were in-depth taped interviews, others were informal conversations. I also distributed a one-page written questionnaire to fifty randomly selected students on two different campuses.

34. For examples of the developing idea that a sweeping critique of patriarchy was necessary see "A Conversation with Virginia Mollenkott," *The Other Side* (May–June 1976): 21–75; Kathleen E. Corley and Karen J. Torjesen, "Sexuality, Hierarchy, and Evangelicalism," *TSF Bulletin* 10, no. 4 (March–April 1987): 23–27; Anne Eggebroten, "Handling Power: Unchristian, Unfeminine, Unkind?" *The Other Side* (December 1986): 20–25.

NOTES TO CHAPTER 2

1. There are related discussions over the degree to which Southern Baptists can be considered fundamentalists. It's helpful to remember that labeling is a form of boundary setting and that various people use these terms in an effort to decide who is "in" and who is "out,"

2. Timothy Weber, interview by author, 14 June, 1995 Louisville, Ky., tape recording.

3. Sometimes they do so in surprising ways. For more on these labels and their uses, see Davis T. Morgan, *The New Crusade, the New Holy Land: Conflict in the Southern Baptist Convention, 1969–1991* (Tuscaloosa: University of Alabama Press, 1996); Arthur Emery Farnsley II, *Southern Baptist Politics* (University Park, Pa.: Pennsylvania State Press, 1994); and Nancy Ammerman, *Baptist Battles* (New Brunswick: Rutgers University Press, 1990). See also David Edwin Harrell Jr., *The Varieties of Southern Evangelicalism* (Macon, Ga.: Mercer University Press, 1981).

4. For an exploration of the relationship between these two groups from the perspective of leaders in each group, see David S. Dockery, ed., *Southern Baptists and American Evangelicals* (Nashville: Broadman and Holman, 1993)

5. For a discussion of the tension-filled relationship between evangelicals and Southern Baptists, and the issues therein, see Barry Hankins, *Uneasy in Babylon: Southern Baptist Conservatives and American Culture* (Tuscaloosa: University of Alabama Press, 2002).

6. Funding from the Society for the Scientific Study of Religion and the Louisville Institute helped with travel and transcription expenses.

7. See Ammerman, *Baptist Battles.* Ammerman argues that the fundamentalists believed the "staff and graduates of three 'liberal' seminaries formed the backbone of their opposition" (243). Many would quibble over the use of the label "liberal" for either side in this controversy; it does seem clear that the seminaries were in the hands of "nonfundamentalists."

8. Bill Leonard, *God's Last and Only Hope: The Fragmentation of the Southern Baptist Convention* (Grand Rapids, Mich.: William B. Eerdmans, 1990).

9. Ammerman, *Baptist Battles,* 93.

10. Ibid., 80.

11. The issue was, specifically, whether women could serve as pastors. "Ordination," as a term, is problematic because all Christians do not understand ordination in the same way. While many in this conflict used the terms "women's ordination," Mohler took issue with it. For Mohler, the defining issue is the issue of women serving as head pastor. However, this does not imply that Mohler believes that women can serve as pastors in subordinate pastoral roles; in Mohler's view, only the head pastor is a pastor.

12. Farnsley, *Southern Baptist Politics,* xi.

13. It is difficult to decide what to call these two camps. Some want to label the

conflict as between fundamentalists against conservatives; others prefer fundamentalists/conservatives against moderates. Also, for fuller examination of the controversies on each of the seminary campuses, see Ammerman, Leonard, and Farnsley.

14. Hankins, *Uneasy in Babylon*.

15. Ibid., 75.

16. This is drawn from my interview with Timothy Weber, one of the five new faculty member hired in 1992 and confirmed in an article by Bill Wolfe, "Baptist Trustees Approve 5 Teachers for Seminary, Disapprove of Views," *Courier Journal*, 30 April 1992.

17. A copy of Sherwood's statement was made available to me by Marvin Knox, editor of the *Western Recorder* in Louisville.

18. This synopsis was constructed from newspaper accounts, my interviews, and various documents provided to me by those with whom I talked.

19. The information contained in this update were provided by Garland in a letter to the author dated 30 December 2001.

20. Timothy Weber, interview by author, 14 June 1995, Louisville, Ky., tape recording.

21. As a student, he signed a petition endorsing women pastors, a view he has since repudiated. When questioned on the reversal in an interview, he merely said that he had changed his mind.

22. Wolfe, *Courier Journal*, 30 April 1992.

23. David Dockery, interview by author, 15 June, 1995, Louisville, Ky., tape recording.

24. Wolfe, *Courier Journal*.

25. Even if this story is but a rumor, it illustrates the general perception of Mohler's attitude and demeanor.

NOTES TO CHAPTER 3

1. James Davidson Hunter, *Evangelicalism: The Coming Generation* (Chicago: University of Chicago Press, 1987), 76–115.

2. Lisa R. Avalos-Bock, "Authority, Credibility, and Hearing God's Voice: Barriers to Women's Full Inclusion in a Contemporary Protestant Church," paper presented at the annual meeting of the Society for the Scientific Study of Religion, St. Louis, Missouri, October 1995, 16, 17.

3. Her male partner's title did not include the prefix "co-."

4. The names of my interview subjects and the institutions with which they are (or were) affiliated have been changed to protect their identities.

5. I was able to corroborate this claim in various ways. In some cases, the women I interviewed shared teaching evaluations with me, and, in other cases, I interviewed students. I was able to look at the school paper's chronicle of one

conflict (and to assess what students said about the teacher under fire), in another case, I was shown an extensive file of letters of support from students.

6. Debra L. Sequeira, Thomas Trzyna, Martin L. Abbott, and Delbert S. McHenry, "'The Kingdom Has Not Yet Come': Coping with Microinequities within a Christian University," *Research on Christian Higher Education* 2 (1995): 9.

7. From the report issued by Committee of the American Association of University Professors, printed in *Academe*, AAUP, Washington, D.C., September–October 1999.

8. Sequeira et al., "'The Kingdom Has Not Yet Come,'" 7–9.

9. The names of the students, faculty members, and institutions have been changed.

10. Margaret Lamberts Bendroth dates this practice to the 1930s and argues that, at least at that point, the purpose of the limiting the number of women students was to keep the feminization of Christianity at bay. See Bendroth, *Fundamentalism and Gender, 1875 to the Present* (New Haven: Yale University Press, 1993), 91–92.

11. See Susan Faludi, *Backlash: The Undeclared War against American Women* (New York: Doubleday, 1991), for an exploration of the reported backlash against feminism in the larger secular culture.

12. Hunter, *Evangelicalism*.

13. Bendroth, *Fundamentalism and Gender*, 75.

14. Anne Hutchinson and Roger Williams were colonial Puritans both of whom took the Reformation conviction about believers' direct access to God to its logical conclusion and were banished from the Massachusetts Bay Colony for doing so. In many ways, their stories are similar.

15. The student believed that this was a particularly serious problem for religious studies majors because this major is often seen as preparation for seminary and the ministry.

16. The Center for Christian Women in Leadership, based at Eastern College, in Pennsylvania, recognized this problem and organized a conference to explore the issues relating to mentoring. The center brought together female faculty and students to put together structured mentoring programs in their respective Christian colleges.

17. It is very important to note here that none of the stories on which I am reporting resulted in charges being brought. At times this was an institutional failing, because women complained and nothing was done. More often, however, the women involved did not even raise the issue with anyone in authority. The result is, of course, that the accused had no opportunity to challenge the accusations. But, again, whether or not sexual harassment could be proved in each of the cases, what is relevant to this study is the issues around the perceived harassment and not the guilt or innocence of those accused.

18. One such admission was part of a public lecture of which I have a "bootleg" audiotape in my files.

19. It seems necessary to reiterate two caveats. First, I make no claims that these respondents constituted a random sample and do not draw conclusions as to how widespread these problems are. I do know that these problems are not experienced by all women on these campuses and that they do not shape the entire experience of college life for those who do experience them. At the same time, however, I did find similar stories repeated again and again. I found them in every context I studied. I met people who knew the nature of my study by word of mouth (it is a small community) and who told me their own stories and secondhand stories of friends and colleagues that matched others I had found.

20. Virginia Hearn, *Our Struggle to Serve: The Stories of fifteen Evangelical Women* (Waco: Word Books, 1979).

21. For studies on the relationship between authoritarian religious views and abuse, see Margaret J. Rinck, *Christian Men Who Hate Women: Healing Hurting Relationships* (Grand Rapids, Mich.: Zondervan, 1990), and Donald Capps, "Religion and Child Abuse: Perfect Together," *Journal for the Scientific Study of Religion* 31, no. 2 (March 1992): 1–14.

22. Virginia Ramey Mollenkott in Hearn, *Our Struggle to Serve*, 160.

NOTES TO CHAPTER 4

1. Betty DeBerg, *Ungodly Women: Gender and the First Wave of American Fundamentalism* (Minneapolis: Fortress Press, 1990.)

2. Nancy Ammerman, *Baptist Battles: Social Change and Religious Conflict in the Southern Baptist Convention* (New Brunswick: Rutgers University Press, 1990).

3. For other examples of the exploration of strong antifeminism, see James Davison Hunter, *Culture Wars: The Struggle to Define American* (San Francisco: Basic Books, 1991) and Nancy Ammerman, *Bible Believers: Fundamentalists in the Modern World* (New Brunswick, N.J.: Rutgers University Press, 1987).

4. James Davison Hunter, *Evangelicalism: The Coming Generation* (Chicago: University of Chicago Press, 1987).

5. Judith Stacey, *Brave New Families: Stories of Domestic Upheaval in Late-Twentieth-Century America* (San Francisco: Basic Books, 1990). A few historians have also examined evangelical feminism. See Margaret Lamberts Bendroth, *Fundamentalism and Gender, 1875 to the Present* (New Haven: Yale University Press, 1993); Janette Hassey, *No Time for Silence: Evangelical Women in Public Ministry around the Turn of the Century* (Grand Rapids, Mich.: Academie Books, 1986); and Nancy A. Hardesty, *Women Called to Witness: Evangelical Feminism in the 19th Century* (Nashville: Abingdon Books, 1984).

6. Judith Stacey and Elizabeth Susan Gerard, "'We Are Not Doormats': The

Influence of Feminism on Contemporary Evangelicals in the United States," in *Uncertain Terms: Negotiating Gender in American Culture,* ed. Faye Ginsburg and Anna Lowenhaupt Tsing (Boston: Beacon Press, 1990).

7. Stacey and Gerard, "'We Are Not Doormats,'" 111.

8. See, for example, Donald Dayton, *Discovering an Evangelical Heritage* (Peabody, Mass.: Hendrickson, 1976).

9. For discussions of cultural-production theory, see Robert Wuthnow and Marcia Witten, "New Directions in the Study of Culture," *Annual Review of Sociology* (Palo Alto, Calif.: Annual Reviews, 1988); Wuthnow, *Rediscovering the Sacred: Perspectives on Religion in Contemporary Society* (Grand Rapids, Mich.: William B. Eerdmans, 1992); and Wuthnow, *Producing the Sacred: An Essay on Public Religion* (Chicago: University of Illinois Press, 1994).

10. Wuthnow, *Producing the Sacred,* 28.

11. Wuthnow, *Rediscovering the Sacred,* 52.

12. Ibid.

13. Ibid., 53.

14. Ibid., 54–55.

15. Ibid., 54.

16. Ibid., 56.

17. David Chidester and Edward T. Linenthal, eds., *American Sacred Space* (Bloomington: Indiana University Press, 1995).

18. Ibid., 5.

19. While the theoretical volume in which Chidester and Linenthal most clearly lay out their conflict theory concerns sacred space, the argument clearly applies to notions of the sacred more generally. Furthermore, as is argued in the next section, the human body can be understood as symbolic space, in which case conflict over gender can be viewed as conflict over sacred space.

20. Chidester and Linenthal, *American Sacred Space,* 9.

21. Ibid., 12.

22. Ibid., 15.

23. Ibid., 24.

24. Hunter, *Culture Wars.*

25. James Davison Hunter, *Before the Shooting Begins: Searching for Democracy in America's Culture War* (New York: Free Press, 1994).

26. Pew Charitable Trusts have funded an ongoing project, overseen by Douglass Jacobson and William Trollinger, at Messiah College, the focus of which is to critique the culture wars thesis and to develop an alternative framework that focuses on those who don't fit into either side of Hunter's culture war.

27. See, for example, Nancy J. Davis and Robert T. Robinson, "Religious Orthodoxy in American Society: The Myth of a Monolithic Camp," *Journal for the Scientific Study of Religion* 35, no. 3 (September 1996): 229–245.

28. For a more thorough discussion of this "two-party paradigm," see Martin

Marty, *Righteous Empire: The Protestant Experience in America* (New York: Dial Press, 1970), 177–198. Marty credits a former graduate student, Jean Miller Schmidt, with this idea and the label for it, which she put forth in her unpublished doctoral dissertation at the University of Chicago.

29. James Davison Hunter "Response to Davis and Robinson: Remembering Durkheim," *Journal for the Scientific Study of Religion* 35, no. 3 (September 1996): 246–248.

30. Jackson Carroll and Penny Long Marler, "Culture Wars? Insights from Ethnographies of Two Protestant Seminaries," *Sociology of Religion* 56, no. 1 (spring 1995): 1–20.

31. Carroll and Marler. "Culture Wars."

32. James Davison Hunter and Kimon Howland Sargeant, "Religion, Women, and the Transformation of Public Culture," *Social Research* 60, no. 3 (fall 1993): 545–570.

33. Judith Butler, *Gender Trouble: Feminism and the Subversion of Identity* (New York: Routledge, 1999).

34. Ibid., 33.

35. For examples of sociological studies that explore the significance of conflict for cultural-production models see Fred Kniss, "Ideas and Symbols as Resources in Intra-religious Conflict: The Case of American Mennonites," *Sociology of Religion* 57, no. 1 (1996): 7–23; Gene Burns, "Studying the Political Culture of American Catholicism," *Sociology of Religion* 57, no. 1 (1996): 37–53; David Swartz, "Bridging the Study of Culture and Religion: Pierre Bourdieu's Political Economy of Symbolic Power," *Sociology of Religion* 57, no. 1 (1996): 71–85.

36. See Hunter, *Evangelicalism: The Coming Generation.*

37. Wuthnow, *Rediscovering the Sacred*, 48.

38. Ibid.

NOTES TO CHAPTER 5

1. Cited in Colleen McDannell, *The Christian Home in Victorian America, 1840–1900* (Bloomington: Indiana University Press, 1986), 24.

2. See Robert Wuthnow, *Sharing the Journey* (New York: Free Press, 1994). Wuthnow found that 40 percent of Americans report being members of small groups, most of which are religious in nature.

3. This overview was compiled from observations made during visits to women's meetings and conversations with men and women about what takes place at their respective meetings.

4. Mary Stewart Van Leeuwen, "Servanthood or Soft Patriarchy? A Christian Feminist Looks at the Promise Keepers Movement," *Journal of Men's Studies*, forthcoming.

5. Tony Evans, "Spiritual Purity," in *Seven Promises of a Promise Keeper* ed. Al Janssen(Colorado Springs: Focus on the Family, 1994), 79–80.

6. Rebecca Merrill Groothuis and Douglas Groothuis, "Women Keep Promises Too!" *Perspectives: A Journal of Reformed Thought* 10, (August–September 1995): 19–20.

7. The connection between multilevel marketing and evangelical Christianity is an intriguing one. Evangelicals are involved in many multilevel-marketing organizations, including Amway, Mary Kay Cosmetics, and Herbalife.

8. John Piper and Wayne Grudem, *Rediscovering Biblical Manhood and Womanhood* (Wheaton, Ill.: Crossway Books, 1993), 273.

9. Stephen B. Clark, *Man and Woman in Christ: An Examination of the Roles of Men and Women in Light of Scripture and the Social Sciences* (Ann Arbor Mich.: Servant Books, 1980), 286.

10. For examples of evangelical feminist works that attempt to recapture the history of Christianity see Janette Hassey, *No Time for Silence: Evangelical Women in Public Ministry around the Turn of the Century* (Grand Rapids, Mich.: Zondervan, 1986); Nancy A. Hardesty, *Women Called to Witness: Evangelical Feminism in the Nineteenth Century* (Nashville: Abingdon Press, 1984); Letha Dawson Scanzoni and Nancy A. Hardesty, *All We're Meant to Be: Biblical Feminism for Today* (Grand Rapids, Mich.: William B. Eerdmans, 1992).

11. Janette Hassey, *No Time for Silence: Evangelical Women in Public Ministry around the Turn of the Century* (Grand Rapids, Mich.: Academie Books, 1986). Margaret Lamberts Bendroth, *Fundamentalism and Gender, 1875 to the Present* (New Haven: Yale University Press, 1993).

12. Hassey, *No Time for Silence*, 31.

13. Jessie Penn-Lewis, *The Magna Charta of Women* (Minneapolis: Bethany Fellowship, 1975).

14. Hassey, *No Time for Silence*, 114.

15. For expansion of this argument, see Bendroth, *Fundamentalism and Gender*.

16. Martin Riesebrodt, "Fundamentalism and the Political Mobilization of Women," in *The Political Dimensions of Religion*, ed. Said Amir Arjomano (Albany: State University of New York Press, 1993).

17. Colleen McDannell, *Material Christianity: Religion and Popular Culture in America* (New Haven: Yale University Press, 1995), 4.

18. Ibid., 57.

19. Ibid.

20. In McDannell's example, a Mormon woman who considers herself a liberal wears her sacred garments and says, "Then those women and those people in that church cannot put me is some weird category because obviously I'm a member."

21. Ibid., 164.

22. Barbara Wheeler, "You Who Were Far Off: Religious Divisions and the Role

of Religious Research," Douglass Lecture, presented to the Religious Research Association, St. Louis, Missouri, October 1995, 14.

23. The research for this chapter included lengthy visits to several Christian bookstores in Maine, Pennsylvania, Kentucky, Virginia, and California, as well as visits to various church services and interviews with evangelicals. I also draw on observations made during the years in which I was a member of several evangelical churches in several different states.

24. See Randall Balmer, *Mine Eyes Have Seen the Glory: A Journey into the Evangelical Subculture in America* (New York: Oxford University Press, 1989).

25. Wheeler, "You Who Were Far Off," 8.

26. It is interesting to note that while the *Left Behind* novels—and the earlier Frank Peretti novels-are "fictionalized," to those shopping at Christian bookstores they are anything but fiction.

27. The March 7, 1994, issue of *Publishers Weekly* indicated that, in the Christian book industry, in 1993, the two types of books that sold the most copies were books about angels and "niche Bibles."

28. Robert Wuthnow, *Rediscovering the Sacred: Perspectives on Religion in Contemporary Society* (Grand Rapids: William B. Eerdmans, 1992), 47.

29. Ibid.

30. David Chidester and Edward T. Linenthal, eds. *American Sacred Space* (Bloomington: Indiana University Press, 1995), 9.

31. Ibid., 12.

32. Ibid., 16.

33. See Bruce Lincoln, *Discourse and the Construction of Society* (Oxford: Oxford University Press, 1989).

34. Wuthnow, *Rediscovering the Sacred*, 44.

NOTES TO CHAPTER 6

1. Susan Faludi, *Backlash: The Undeclared War Against American Women* (New York: Doubleday, 1991).

2. For a detailed study of the ebbs and flows of conservative support for women's public roles in evangelism see Margaret Lamberts Bendroth *Fundamentalism and Gender, 1875 to the Present* (New Haven: Yale University Press, 1993).

3. The reference is to Abraham Kuyper, the Dutch Reformed theologian (1837–1920). Kuyper held that Calvinist Christianity was a political and social system as well as a religious one and that no aspect of life could be separated from religion.

4. Mark Chaves and James Cavendish, "Social Movements and Organizational Change," paper presented at the annual meeting of the Society for the Scientific Study of Religion, St. Louis, Missouri, 1995, and Mark Chaves, *Ordaining Women:*

Culture and Conflict in Religious Organizations (Cambridge, Mass.: Harvard University Press, 1997).

5. For an exploration of similar transformations concerning what it means to be a feminist that have occurred in the larger culture see Ruth Rosen, *The World Split Open: How the Modern Women's Movement Changed America* (New York: Viking Penguin, 2000).

6. While I contend that this is the case in the context of American Protestant fundamentalism, I make no argument that this is necessarily so in other cultural contexts.

NOTES TO THE CONCLUSION

1. James Davison Hunter, "Response to Davis and Robinson: Remembering Durkheim," *Journal for the Scientific Study of Religion* 35, no. 3 (September 1996): 246.

2. David Chidester and Edward Linenthal, *American Sacred Space* (Bloomington: Indiana University Press, 1995).

3. See Russell T. McCutcheon, *The Insider-Outsider Problem in the Study of Religion* (London: Cassell, 1999).

4. To cite just a few of the many examples: Christel Manning, *God Gave us the Right* (New Brunswick: Rutgers University Press, 1999); Brenda Brasher, *Godly Women* (New Brunswick: Rutgers University Press, 1998); and R. Marie Griffith, *God's Daughters* (Berkeley: University of California Press, 1998), examine these issues in conservative Christian contexts. In related studies, Debra Kaufman, *Rachel's Daughters* (New Brunswick: Rutgers University Press, 1991), and Lynn Davidman, *Tradition in a Rootless World* (Berkeley: University of California Press, 1991), explore the stories of women who convert to Orthodox Judaism.

5. Randall Balmer, "American Fundamentalism: The Ideal of Femininity," in *Fundamentalism and Gender*, ed. John Stratton Hawley (Oxford: Oxford University Press, 1994), 58.

6. Karen McCarthy Brown, "Fundamentalism and the Control of Women," in *Fundamentalism and Gender*, ed. John Stratton Hawley (Oxford: Oxford University Press, 1994), 175–189.

7. Karen Torjesen, interview by author, 17 February 1995, Los Angeles, Calif., tape recording.

Bibliography

In addition to sources cited, I have also drawn extensively on the personal files of many of the subjects of my study, to whom I have promised confidentiality.

Primary Sources

Achtemeier, Elizabeth Rice. *The Feminine Crisis in Christian Faith.* New York: Abingdon Press, 1965.

Alsdurf, James. *Battered into Submission: The Tragedy of Wife Abuse in the Christian Home.* Downers Grove, Ill.: InterVarsity Press, 1989.

Alsdurf, Phyllis. "Evangelical Feminists: Ministry Is the Issue." *Christianity Today,* 21 July 1978.

Armstrong, Karen. *The Gospel according to Woman: Christianity's Creation of the Sex War in the West.* Garden City, N.Y.: Anchor Press, 1987.

Balswick, Jack O. *Men at the Crossroads: Beyond Traditional Roles and Modern Options.* Downers Grove, Ill.: InterVarsity Press, 1992.

Balswick, Jack O., and Judith K. Balswick. *The Family: A Christian Perspective on the Contemporary Home.* Grand Rapids, Mich.: Baker Book House, 1991.

Beard, Helen. *Women in the Ministry Today.* Plainfield, N.J.: Logos International, 1980.

Bilezikian, Gilbert G. *Beyond Sex Roles: A Guide for the Study of Female Roles in the Bible.* Grand Rapids, Mich.: Baker Book House, 1985.

Bloesch, Donald G. *Is the Bible Sexist?: Beyond Feminism and Patriarchalism.* Westchester, Ill.: Crossway Books, 1982.

Bordin, Ruth Birgitta Anderson. *Woman and Temperance: The Quest for Power and Liberty, 1873–1900.* Philadelphia: Temple University Press, 1981.

Bourke, Dale Hanson. *"But Can She Type?"* Downers Grove, Ill.: InterVarsity Press, 1986.

Bristow, John Temple. *What Paul Really Said about Women.* San Francisco: Harper and Row, 1988.

Briner, Bob. *Lambs among the Wolves: How Christians Are Influencing American Culture.* Grand Rapids, Mich.: Zondervan, 1995.

Burkett, Larry. *Women Leaving the Workplace: How to Make the Transition from Work to Home.* Chicago: Moody Press, 1995.

Bushnell, Katherine C. *God's Word to Women* privately published 1912, 1923, reprint from God's Word to Women Publishers, Mossville, Ill.

Butler, Diana Hochstedt. "Between Two Worlds." *Christian Century,* 3 March 1993.

Carmody, Denise Lardner. *Feminism and Christianity: A Two-Way Reflection.* Nashville: Abingdon, 1982.

Chittister, Joan. *Women, Ministry, and the Church.* New York: Paulist Press, 1983.

"Christians for Biblical Equality: Members and Friends Survey." St. Paul, Minn.: Christians for Biblical Equality, July 1991.

Christiansen, Winnie. *Caught with My Mouth Open.* Wheaton, Ill.: Harold Shaw, n.d.

Clark, Stephen B. *Man and Woman in Christ: An Examination of the Roles of Men and Women in Light of Scripture.* Ann Arbor: Servant Books, 1980.

Clouse, Bonnidell, and Robert G. Clouse, eds. *Women in Ministry: Four Views.* Downers Grove, Ill.: InterVarsity Press, 1989.

Cook, Barbara. *Ordinary Women, Extraordinary Strength: A Biblical Perspective of Feminine Potential.* Lynnwood, Wash.: Aglow Publications, 1988.

Cook, Kaye V. *Man and Woman Alone and Together.* Wheaton, Ill.: Victor Books, 1992.

Cooper, Darien B. *You Can Be the Wife of a Happy Husband.* Wheaton, Ill.: Victor Books, 1974.

Corley, Kathleen E., and Karen J. Torjesen. "Sexuality, Hierarchy and Evangelicalism." *TSF Bulletin* 10, no. 4 (March–April 1987): 23–27.

Cowles, C. S. *A Woman's Place: Leadership in the Church.* Kansas City, Mo.: Beacon Hill Press of Kansas City, n.d.

Crabb, Lawrence J. *Men and Women: Enjoying the Difference.* Grand Rapids, Mich.: Zondervan, 1991.

———. *The Silence of Adam: Becoming Men of Courage in a World of Chaos.* Grand Rapids, Mich.: Zondervan, 1995.

Dobson, James. *Prescription for a Tired Housewife.* Wheaton, Ill.: Tyndale House, 1975.

———. *Marriage and Sexuality: Dr. Dobson Answers Your Questions.* Wheaton, Ill.: Tyndale House, 1982.

Dockery, David. *Southern Baptists and American Evangelicals.* Nashville: Broadman and Holman, 1993.

Eggebroten, Anne. "Handling Power: Unchristian, Unfeminine, Unkind?" *The Other Side,* December 1986, 20–25.

"Evangelical Feminism." *Post American,* August–September 1974, 3–29.

Evans, Mary J. *Woman in the Bible: An Overview of All the Crucial Passages on Woman's Roles.* Downer's Grove: Ill.: InterVarsity Press, 1984.

Faludi, Susan. *Backlash: The Undeclared War against American Women.* New York: Doubleday, 1991.

Finger, Lareta Halteman. "Women in Pulpits." *The Other Side,* July 1979, 14–27.

"Focus on the Family" radio broadcast transcript. "Biblical Masculinity and Femininity," James Dobson interview of Wayne Grudem and Mary Kassian. 9, 10 March 1992.

Folio: A Newsletter for Southern Baptist Women. Center for Women in Ministry, Louisville, Kentucky, Autumn 1984–Summer 1994.

Free Indeed, March–April 1978 through June–July 1979.

Garland, Diana. "The State of the Carver School of Social Work, March 20,1995." Released by Garland for general distribution.

———. Personal files, including newspaper clippings from *Courier Journal* and *Western Recorder,* press releases, correspondence.

Gilder, George. *Men and Marriage.* Gretna, La.: Pelican, 1986.

Glaz, Maxine, and Jeanne Stevenson Moessner, eds. *Women in Travail and Transition: A New Pastoral Care.* Minneapolis: Fortress Press, 1991.

Green Leaf: Newsletter of the Bay Area Women's Caucus, San Francisco, Spring 1982–Spring 1987.

Grissen, Lillian V. *For Such a Time as This: Twenty-Six Women of Vision and Faith Tell Their Stories.* Grand Rapids, Mich.: William B. Eerdmans, 1991.

Groothuis, Rebecca Merrill. *Women Caught in Conflict: The Culture War between Traditionalism and Feminism.* Grand Rapids, Mich.: Baker Book House, 1994.

Gundry, Patricia. *Woman Be Free: Biblical Equality for Women.* Grand Rapids, Mich.: Zondervan, 1977.

———. *The Complete Woman.* Garden City, N.Y.: Doubleday, 1981.

———. *Neither Slave nor Free: Helping Women Answer the Call to Church Leadership.* San Francisco: Harper and Row, 1987.

Gurko, Miriam. *The Ladies of Seneca Falls: The Birth of the Women's Rights Movement.* New York: Schocken Books, 1976.

Hagan, June Steffensen, ed. *Gender Matters: Women's Studies for the Christian Community.* Grand Rapids, Mich.: Academie Books, 1990.

———. *Rattling Those Dry Bones: Women Changing the Church.* San Diego: Lura Media, 1995.

Hagin, Kenneth E. *The Woman Question.* Greensburg, Pa.: Manna Christian Outreach, 1975.

Hancock, Maxine. *Love, Honor and Be Free.* Chicago: Moody Press, 1975.

Hardesty, Nancy A. "Women: Second-Class Citizens." *Eternity,* January 1971, 14–20.

———. *Great Women of the Faith: The Strength and Influence of Christian Women.* Grand Rapids, Mich.: Baker Book House, 1980.

Hassey, Janette. *No Time for Silence: Evangelical Women in Public Ministry around the Turn of the Century.* Grand Rapids, Mich.: Academie Books, 1986.

Haubert, Katherine M. *Women as Leaders: Accepting the Challenge of Scripture.* Monrovia, Calif.: MARC, 1993.

Hayter, Mary. *The New Eve in Christ: The Use and Abuse of the Bible in the Debate about Women in the Church.* London: SPCK, 1987.

Hearn, Virginia. *Our Struggle to Serve: The Stories of Fifteen Evangelical Women.* Waco, Tex.: Word Books, 1979.

Hicks, Robert. *Men of All Passions: The Conflicting Drives and Complex Desires of a Man of God.* Colorado Springs: NavPress, 1995.

Howe, Margaret E. *Women and Church Leadership.* Grand Rapids, Mich.: Zondervan, 1982.

Hull, Gretchen Gabelein. *Equal to Serve: Women and Men in the Church and Home.* Old Tappan, N.J.: F. H. Revell, 1987.

Hunt, Gladys M. *Ms. Means Myself.* Grand Rapids, Mich.: Zondervan, 1972.

Jakes, T. D. *Woman Thou Art Loosed: Healing the Wounds of the Past.* Shippensburg, Pa.: Treasure House, 1995.

———. *Loose That Man and Let Him Go!* Tulsa: Albury Press, 1995.

Jewett, Paul King. *MAN as Male and Female: A Study in Sexual Relationships from a Theological Point of View.* Grand Rapids, Mich.: William B. Eerdmans, 1975.

———. *The Ordination of Women.* Grand Rapids, Mich.: William B. Eerdmans, 1980.

Karssen, Gien. *The Man Who Was Different: Jesus' Encounters with Women.* Colorado Springs: NavPress, 1987.

Kennedy, Paul. "A Sociological Analysis of Christian Feminism within an Evangelical Christian Seminary Environment." Unpublished manuscript.

Kerr, Clarence W. *God's Pattern for the Home.* Los Angeles: Cowman Publications, 1953.

Kroeger, Richard Clark, and Catherine Clark Kroeger. *Women Clergy . . . Sinners and Servants?* New York: Council on Women and the Church, the United Presbyterian Church in the U.S.A., 1981.

———. *I Suffer Not a Woman: Rethinking 1 Timothy 2:11–15 in Light of Ancient Evidence.* Grand Rapids, Mich.: Baker Book House, 1992.

Laird, Rebecca. *Ordained Women in the Church of the Nazarene.* Kansas City, Mo.: Nazarene Publishing House, n.d.

Landorf, Joyce. *To Lib or Not to Lib.* Wheaton, Ill.: Victor Books, 1974.

Leonard, Juanita Evans, ed. *Called to Minister, Empowered to Serve.* Anderson, Ind.: Warner Press, 1989.

Malcolm, Kari Torjesen. *Women at the Crossroads: A Path beyond Feminism and Traditionalism.* Downers Grove, Ill.: InterVarsity Press, 1982.

Marshall, Molly T. "New Inquisition: Academic Freedom and Women's Religion." Unpublished paper.

Martin, Faith McBurney. *Call Me Blessed: The Emerging Christian Woman.* Grand Rapids, Mich.: William B. Eerdmans, 1988.

Maxwell, Joe. "Dean's Dismissal Draws Faculty, Student Protest." *Christianity Today,* 15 May 1995, 4–55.

Maxwell, L. E., and Ruth C. Dearing. *Women in Ministry.* Wheaton, Ill.: Victor Books, n.d.

Merrill, Rebecca, and Douglas Groothuis, "Women Keep Promises Too!" *Perspectives: A Journal of Reformed Thought* 10, no. 7 (August–September 1995): 19–23.

Mickelsen, Alvera, ed. *Women Authority and the Bible.* Downers Grove, Ill. Inter-Varsity Press, 1986.

Mitchell, Ella Pearson, ed. *To Preach or Not to Preach: Twenty-one Outstanding Black Preachers Say Yes!* Valley Forge, Pa.: Judson Press, 1991.

Mollenkott, Virginia Ramey. "Jesus, Women and the Resurrection." *Eternity,* March 1975, 17–37.

———. "A Conversation with Virginia Mollenkott." *The Other Side,* May–June 1976, 21–75.

———. *Women, Men, and the Bible.* Nashville: Abingdon, 1977.

———. *Speech, Silence, Action!: The Cycle of Faith.* Nashville: Abingdon Press, 1980.

———. *Sensuous Spirituality: Out from Fundamentalism.* New York: Crossroad, 1992.

Morgan, Marabel. *The Total Woman.* New York: Pocket Books, 1975.

Morley, Patrick M. *The Seven Seasons of a Man's Life.* Nashville: Thomas Nelson, 1995.

Narramore, Clyde Morris. *A Woman's World: A Christian Psychologist Discusses Twelve Common Problem Areas.* Grand Rapids, Mich.: Zondervan, 1963.

Neff, Miriam. *Sisters of the Heart: Devotions for Ordinary Women with Extraordinary Challenges.* Nashville: Thomas Nelson, 1995.

———. *Sisters: The Story Goes On. Telling Stories for Hope and Healing.* Nashville: Thomas Nelson, 1996.

Ockenga, Harold John. *Women Who Made Bible History: Messages and Character Sketches Dealing with Familiar Bible Women.* Grand Rapids, Mich.: Zondervan, 1962.

Oddie, William. *What Will Happen to God?: Feminism and the Reconstruction of Christian Belief.* London: SPCK, 1984.

Oinonen, Julie. "Community Disturbed by Departure of Faculty." *The Bagpipe: The Student Newspaper of Covenant College,* Covenant College, Lookout Mountain, Tennessee, 9 April 1993, 1.

Orem, Sara L. "Moving the Mountain: Women in Ministry." M.A. thesis, United Theological Seminary of the Twin Cities, New Brighton, Minnesota, 1992.

Osborn, Daisy Marie Washburn. *Choices for Women Who Win.* Tulsa, Okla.: OSFO, 1986.

————. *Woman and Self-Esteem*. Tulsa, Okla.: OSFO, 1991.

Penn-Lewis, Jessie. *The Magna Charta of Women*. Minneapolis: Bethany Fellowship, 1975.

Piper, John. *What's the Difference?: Manhood and Womanhood Defined according to the Bible*. Wheaton, Ill.: Council on Biblical Manhood and Womanhood, 1989.

————. *Can Our Differences Be Settled? A Detailed Response to the Evangelical Feminist Position Statement of Christians for Biblical Equality*. Wheaton, Ill: Council on Biblical Manhood and Womanhood, 1992.

Piper, John, and Wayne Grudem. *Recovering Biblical Manhood and Womanhood: A Response to Evangelical Feminism*. Wheaton, Ill.: Crossway Books, 1991.

Pride, Mary. *The Way Home: Beyond Feminism and Back to Reality*. Westchester, Ill.: Crossway Books, 1978.

Priscilla Papers. Christians for Biblical Equality, St. Paul, Minnesota, Autumn 1987–Spring 1994.

Proctor, Pam. *Women in the Pulpit: Is God an Equal Opportunity Employer?* Garden City, N.Y.: Doubleday, 1976.

Rice, John R. *Bobbed Hair, Bossy Wives, and Women Preachers*. Murfreesboro, Tenn.: Sword of the Lord Publishers, 1941.

Rinck, Margaret J. *Christian Men Who Hate Women: Healing Hurting Relationships*. Grand Rapids, Mich.: Zondervan, 1990.

Robison, James B., and David Dockery, eds. *Beyond the Impasse? Scripture, Interpretation, and Theology in Baptist Life*. Nashville: Broadman Press, 1992.

Sayers, Dorothy L. *A Matter of Eternity*. Grand Rapids, Mich.: William B. Eerdmans, 1973.

————. "Are Women Human?" *Eternity*, February 1974, 15–18.

Scanzoni, Letha. "Woman's Place: Silence or Service." *Eternity*, February 1966, 14–19.

Scanzoni, Letha Dawson, and Nancy A. Hardesty. *All We're Meant to Be: A Biblical Approach to Women's Liberation*. Waco, Tex.: Word Books, 1974.

————. *All We're Meant to Be: Biblical Feminism for Today*. Grand Rapids, Mich.: William B. Eerdmans, 1992.

Scanzoni, Letha Dawson, and Virginia Ramey Mollenkott. *Is the Homosexual My Neighbor?* San Francisco: Harper San Francisco, 1994.

————. "Elevate Marriage to Partnership." *Eternity*, July 1968, 11–12.

Schaller, Lyle E. *Women as Pastors*. Nashville: Abingdon, 1982.

Schlafly, Phyllis. *The Power of the Christian Woman*. Cincinnati: Standard, 1981.

Schmidt, Alvin J. *Veiled and Silenced: How Culture Shaped Sexist Theology*. Macon, Ga.: Mercer University Press, 1989.

Schmidt, Ruth A. "Second-Class Citizenship in the Kingdom of God." *Christianity Today*, 1 January 1971, 13–14.

Scholer, David M. *A Biblical Basis of Equal Partnership: Women and Men in the*

Ministry of the Church. New York: Ministers and Missionaries Benefit Board of the American Baptist Churches, 1989.

Seven Promises of a Promise Keeper, ed. Al Janssen. Colorado Springs: Focus on the Family Publishing, 1994.

Sherwood, David. "Response Regarding Theological and Biblical Convictions." Unpublished comments, 9 March 1995.

Smith, Charles Ryder. *The Bible Doctrine of Womanhood in Its Historical Evolution.* London: Epworth Press, 1923.

Spencer, Aida Besancon. *Beyond the Curse: Women Called to Ministry.* Nashville: Thomas Nelson, 1985.

Spencer, Aida Besancon, with Donna F. G. Hailson, Catherine Clark Kroeger, and William David Spencer. *The Goddess Revival.* Grand Rapids, Mich.: Baker Books, 1995.

Spring, Beth, and Kelsey Menehan. "Women in Seminary: Preparing for What?" *Christianity Today,* 5 December 1986, 18–23.

Stendahl, Brita K. *The Force of Tradition: A Case Study of Women Priests in Sweden.* Philadelphia: Fortress Press, 1985.

Stephens, Shirley. *A New Testament View of Women.* Nashville: Broadman Press, 1980.

Storkey, Elaine. *What's Right with Feminism.* Grand Rapids, Mich.: William B. Eerdmans, 1986.

Theology News and Notes: Women and Ministry. Pasadena: Fuller Theological Seminary, March 1995.

Theology News and Notes: Women in Transition. Pasadena: Fuller Theological Seminary, June 1975.

Thomson, Rosemary. *The Price of Liberty.* Carol Streams, Ill.: Creation House, 1978.

"The Totalled Woman: An Interview with Marabel Morgan. *The Wittenberg Door,* no. 26 (August–September 1975): 7–36.

Trombley, Charles. *Who Said Women Can't Teach?* South Plainfield, N.J.: Bridge, 1985.

Tucker, Ruth. *Daughters of the Church: Women in Ministry from New Testament Times to the Present.* Grand Rapids, Mich.: Academie Books, 1987.

———. *Private Lives of Pastors' Wives.* Grand Rapids, Mich.: Zondervan, 1988.

———. *Multiple Choices.* Grand Rapids, Mich.: Zondervan, 1992.

———. *Women in the Maze: Questions and Answers on Biblical Equality.* Downers Grove, Ill.: InterVarsity Press, 1992.

Update: Newsletter of the Evangelical Women's Caucus. Evangelical Women's Caucus, San Francisco, September 1980–Winter 1994.

Van Leeuwen, Mary Stewart. "The Christian Mind and the Challenge of Gender Relations." *Reformed Journal* 37 (September 1987): 17–23.

————. *Gender and Grace: Love Work and Parenting in a Changing World.* Downers Grove, Ill.: InterVarsity Press, 1990.

————. "Re-inventing the Ties That Bind: Feminism and the Family at the Close of the Twentieth Century," in *Religion, Feminism, and the Family: Studies in Family, Religion, and Culture,* ed. Mary Stewart Van Leeuwen and Anne E. Carr. Philadelphia: Westminster John Knox Press, 1996.

————. "Servanthood or Soft Patriarchy? A Christian Feminist Looks at the Promise Keepers Movement." *Journal of Men's Studies,* forthcoming.

Van Leeuwen, Mary Stewart, ed. *After Eden: Facing the Challenge of Gender Reconciliation.* Grand Rapids, Mich.: William B. Eerdmans, 1993.

Wagner, E. Glenn. *The Awesome Power of Shared Beliefs: Five Things Every Man Should Know.* Dallas: Word Publishing, 1995.

Western Recorder. Kentucky Baptist Convention, Louisville, Kentucky, 30 August 1994–9 May 1995.

Westmont Horizon. Westmont College, Santa Barbara, California, 13 January 1995–29 April 1995.

Williams, Don. *The Apostle Paul and Women in the Church.* Ventura, Calif.: 1980.

"Women in Leadership: Finding Ways to Serve the Church." *Christianity Today* 3 October 1986, 3–30.

Secondary Sources

Ammerman, Nancy Tatom. *Bible Believers: Fundamentalists and the Modern World.* New Brunswick: Rutgers University Press, 1987.

————. *Baptist Battles: Social Change and Religious Conflict in the Southern Baptist Convention.* New Brunswick: Rutgers University Press, 1990.

Avalos-Bock, Lisa. "Authority, Credibility, and Hearing God's Voice: Barriers to Women's Full Inclusion in a Contemporary Protestant Church." Paper presented at the annual meeting of the Society for the Scientific Study of Religion, St. Louis, Missouri, October 1995.

Balmer, Randall. *Mine Eyes Have Seen the Glory: A Journey into the Evangelical Subculture in America.* New York: Oxford University Press, 1989.

Barfoot, Charles, and Gerald Sheppard. "Prophetic vs. Priestly Religion: The Changing Role of Women in Classical Pentecostal Churches." *Review of Religious Research* 22, no. 1: 2–17.

Bendroth, Margaret Lamberts. *Fundamentalism and Gender, 1875 to the Present.* New Haven: Yale University Press, 1993.

Bennion, Janet. *Women of Principle: Female Networking in Contemporary Mormon Polygyny.* Oxford: Oxford University Press, 1998.

Berger, Peter L. *The Sacred Canopy.* Garden City, N.Y.: Doubleday, 1969.

Berger, Peter, and Thomas Luckmann. *The Social Construction of Reality.* New York: Doubleday, 1989.

Bloch, Howard R. *Medieval Misogyny and the Invention of Western Romantic Love.* Chicago: University of Chicago Press, 1991.

Brasher, Brenda. *Godly Women: Fundamentalism and Female Power.* New Brunswick: Rutgers University Press, 1998.

Brereton, Virginia Lieson. "United and Slighted: Women as Subordinate Insiders." In *Between the Times: The Travail of the Protestant Establishment in America, 1900–1960,* ed. W. R. Hutchison. Cambridge: Cambridge University Press, 1989.

Brown, Joanne Carleson, and Carole R. Bohn. *Christianity, Patriarchy, and Abuse: A Feminist Critique.* Cleveland: Pilgrim Press, 1989.

Brown, Karen McCarthy. "Fundamentalism and the Control of Women." In *Fundamentalism and Gender,* ed. John Stratton Hawley. Oxford: Oxford University Press, 1994, 175–189.

Brown, Ruth Murray. "In Defense of Traditional Values: The Anti-Feminist Movement." *Marriage and Family Review* 7, no. 3/4 (fall–winter): 19–35.

Burns, Gene. "Studying the Political Culture of American Catholicism." *Sociology of Religion* 57, no. 1 (spring 1996): 37–53.

Butler, Judith. *Gender Trouble: Feminism and the Subversion of Identity.* New York: Routledge, 1999.

Caplan, Paula J. *Lifting a Ton of Feathers: A Woman's Guide to Surviving in the Academic World.* Toronto: University of Toronto Press, 1993.

Capps, Donald. "Religion and Child Abuse: Perfect Together." *Journal for the Scientific Study of Religion* 31, no. 2 (March 1992): 1–14.

Carroll, Jackson, and Penny Long Marker. "Culture Wars? Insights from Ethnographies of Two Protestant Seminaries." *Sociology of Religion* 56, no. 1 (spring 1995): 1–20.

Charlton, Joy. "What It Means to Go First: Clergywomen of the Pioneer Generation." Paper presented at the annual meeting of the Society for the Scientific Study of Religion, St. Louis, Missouri, October 1995.

Chaves, Mark. *Ordaining Women: Culture and Conflict in Religious Organizations.* Cambridge, Mass.: Harvard University Press, 1997.

Chaves, Mark, and James Cavendish. "Social Movements and Organizational Change: Conflicts over Women's Ordination." Paper presented at the annual meeting of the Society for the Scientific Study of Religion, St. Louis, Missouri, October 1995.

Chidester, David, and Edward Tabor Linenthal, eds. *American Sacred Space.* Bloomington: Indiana University Press, 1995.

Davidman, Lynn. *Tradition in a Rootless World: Women Turn to Orthodox Judaism.* Berkeley: University of California Press, 1991.

Dayton, Donald. *Discovering an Evangelical Heritage.* Peabody, Mass.: Hendrickson, 1976.

Davis, Nancy J., and Robert T. Robinson. "Religious Orthodoxy in American

Society: The Myth of a Monolithic Camp." *Journal for the Scientific Study of Religion* 35, no. 3 (September 1996): 229–245.

DeBerg, Betty. *Ungodly Women: Gender and the First Wave of American Fundamentalism.* Minneapolis: Fortress Press, 1990.

Donovan, Brian. "Re-scripting Masculinity: A Discourse Analysis of the Promise Keepers." Unpublished paper.

Epstein, Barbara Leslie. *The Politics of Domesticity: Women, Evangelism, and Temperance in the Nineteenth Century America.* Middletown, Conn.: Wesleyan University Press, 1981.

Faludi Susan. *Backlash: The Undeclared War against American Women.* New York: Doubleday, 1991.

Farnsley, Arthur Emery II. *Southern Baptist Politics: Authority and Power in the Restructuring of an American Denomination.* University Park, Pa.: Pennsylvania State University, 1994.

Fowler, Robert Booth. "Feminist and Antifeminist Debate within Evangelical Protestantism." *Women and Politics* 5, no. 2/3, (summer–fall 1985): 7–39.

Frank, Douglas W. *Less Than Conquerors: How Evangelicals Entered the Twentieth Century.* Grand Rapids, Mich.: William B. Eerdmans, 1986.

Geertz, Clifford. *The Interpretation of Cultures.* New York: Basic Books, 1973.

Ginsberg, Faye, and Anna Lowenhaupt Tsing, eds. *Uncertain Terms: Negotiating Gender in American Culture.* Boston: Beacon Press, 1990.

———. "Women, Public Ministry, and Fundamentalism, 1920–1950." *Religion and American Culture* 3, no. 2 (summer 1993): 171–196.

Griffith, R. Marie. *God's Daughters: Evangelical Women and the Power of Submission.* Berkeley: University of California Press, 1997.

Hankins, Barry. *Uneasy in Babylon: Southern Baptist Conservatives and American Culture.* Tuscaloosa: University of Alabama Press, 2002.

Hardesty, Nancy A. *Women Called to Witness: Evangelical Feminism in the Nineteenth Century.* Nashville: Abingdon Press, 1984.

Harding, Susan. *The Book of Jerry Falwell.* Princeton: Princeton University Press, 2000.

Harrell, David E., Jr. *Varieties of Southern Evangelicalism.* Macon, Ga.: Mercer University Press, 1981.

Hassey, Janette. *No Time for Silence: Evangelical Women in Public Ministry around the Turn of the Century.* Grand Rapids, Mich.: Academie Books, 1986.

Hawley, John Stratton, ed. *Fundamentalism and Gender.* Oxford: Oxford University Press, 1994.

Himmelstein, Jerome. "The Social Basis of Antifeminism." *Journal for the Scientific Study of Religion* 25, no. 1 (March 1986): 1–15.

Hunter, James Davison. *Evangelicalism: The Coming Generation.* Chicago: University of Chicago, 1987.

————. *Culture Wars: The Struggle to Define America*. San Francisco: Basic Books, 1991.

————. *Before the Shooting Begins: Searching for Democracy in America's Culture War*. New York: Free Press, 1994.

————. "Response to Davis and Robinson: Remembering Durkheim." *Journal for the Scientific Study of Religion* 35, no. 3 (September 1996): 246–248.

Hunter, James Davison, and Kimon Howland Sargeant. "Religion, Women, and the Transformation of Public Culture." *Social Research* 60, no. 3 (fall 1993): 545–570.

Ingram, Larry C., and Ann Carol King. "Organizational Mission as Source of Vulnerability: Comparing Attitudes of Trustees and Professors in Southern Baptist Colleges." *Review of Religious Research* 36, no. 4 (June 1995): 355–368.

Kaufman, Debra Renee. *Rachel's Daughters: Newly Orthodox Jewish Women*. New Brunswick: Rutgers University Press, 1991.

Kitch, Sally L. *Chaste Liberation: Celibacy and Female Cultural Status*. Chicago: University of Illinois Press, 1989.

Kniss, Fred. "Ideas and Symbols as Resources in Intra-religious Conflict: The Case of American Mennonites." *Sociology of Religion* 57, no. 1 (spring 1996): 7–23.

Leonard, Bill J. *God's Last and Only Hope: The Fragmentation of the Southern Baptist Convention*. Grand Rapids, Mich.: William B. Eerdmans, 1990.

————. "Seminary Crackdown: Disputes Intensify in Louisville." *Christian Century*, 10 May 1995, 500–503.

Lawless, Elaine. *Handmaidens of the Lord: Pentecostal Women Preachers and Traditional Religion*. Philadelphia: University of Pennsylvania Press, 1988.

Lehman, Edward. *Women Clergy: Breaking through Gender Barriers*. New Brunswick: Transaction Books, 1985.

Lienesch, Michael. *Redeeming America: Piety and Politics in the Christian Right*. Chapel Hill: University of North Carolina Press, 1993.

Lincoln, Bruce. *Discourse and the Construction of Society*. Oxford: Oxford University Press, 1989.

Manning, Christel. *God Gave Us the Right: Conservative Catholic, Evangelical Protestant, and Orthodox Jewish Women Grapple with Feminism*. New Brunswick: Rutgers University Press, 1999.

Marsden, George. *Fundamentalism and American Culture: The Shaping of Twentieth-Century Evangelicalism, 1870–1925*. Oxford: Oxford University Press, 1980.

————. *Reforming Fundamentalism: Fuller Seminary and the New Evangelicalism*. Grand Rapids, Mich.: William B. Eerdmans, 1987.

————. *Understanding Fundamentalism and Evangelicalism*. Grand Rapids, Mich.: William B. Eerdmans, 1991.

Marsden, George, ed. *Evangelicalism and Modern America*. Grand Rapids, Mich.: William B. Eerdmans, 1984.

Marty, Martin. *Righteous Empire: The Protestant Experience in America*. New York: Dial Press, 1970.

Marty, Martin, and R. Scott Appleby. *The Glory and the Power: The Fundamentalist Challenge to the Modern World*. Boston: Beacon Press, 1992.

Maxwell, Carol J. C., and Ted G. Jelen. "Commandos for Christ: Narratives of Male Pro-Life Activists." Paper presented at the annual meeting of the Association for the Sociology of Religion, Los Angeles, August 1994.

McCutcheon, Russell T. *The Insider–Outsider Problem in the Study of Religion*. London: Cassell, 1999.

McDannell, Colleen. *The Christian Home in Victorian America, 1840–1900*. Bloomington: Indiana University Press, 1986.

———. *Material Christianity: Religion and Popular Culture in America*. New Haven: Yale University Press, 1995.

Moberg, David O. *The Great Reversal: Evangelism versus Social Concern*. Philadelphia: J. B. Lippincott, 1972.

Mueller, William A. *A History of Southern Baptist Seminary*. Nashville: Broadman Press, 1959.

Pevey, Caroline. "Submission and Power among Southern Baptist Ladies." Paper presented at the annual meeting of the Society for the Scientific Study of Religion, Albuquerque, November 1994.

Putney, Gail J., and Snell Putney. *The Adjusted American*. New York: Harper and Row, 1964.

Quebedeaux, Richard. *The Young Evangelicals: The Story of the Emergence of a New Generation of Evangelicals*. New York: Harper and Row, 1974.

———. *The Worldly Evangelicals: Has Success Spoiled America's Born-Again Christians?* San Francisco: Harper and Row, 1978.

Riesebrodt, Martin. *Pious Passion: The Emergence of Modern Fundamentalism in the United States and Iran*. Berkeley: University of California Press, 1990.

———. "Fundamentalism and the Political Mobilization of Women." In *The Political Dimensions of Religion*, ed. Said Amir Arjomano. Albany: SUNY Press, 1993.

Roof, Wade Clark. *A Generation of Seekers: The Spiritual Journeys of the Baby Boom Generation*. San Francisco: HarperCollins, 1993.

Rose, Susan. "Women Warriors: Negotiating Gender in a Charismatic Community." *Sociological Analysis* 48, no. 3 (1987): 245–258.

Rosen, Ruth. *The World Split Open: How the Modern Women's Movement Changed America*. New York: Viking Penguin, 2000.

Schur, Edwin M. *Labeling Women Deviant*. New York: McGraw-Hill, 1984.

Sequeira, Debra L., Thomas Trayna, Martin L. Abbott, and Delbert S. McHenry. "The Kingdom Has Not Yet Come: Coping with Microinequities within a Christian University." *Research on Christian Higher Education* 2 (1995): 1–35.

Stacey, Judith. *Brave New Families: Stories of Domestic Upheaval in Late Twentieth-Century America*. San Francisco: Basic Books, 1990.

Stacey, Judith, and Susan Elizabeth Gerard. "'We Are Not Doormats': The Influence of Feminism on Contemporary Evangelicals in the United States." In *Uncertain Terms: Negotiating Gender in American Culture*, ed. Faye Ginsberg and Anna Lowenhaupt Tsing. Boston: Beacon Press, 1990.

Stanley, Susie C. "'Bumping' into Modernity: Primitive/Modern Tensions in the Wesleyan/Holiness Movement." In *The Primitive Church in the Modern World*, ed. Richard T. Hughes. Chicago: University of Illinois Press, 1995.

Swartz, David. "Bridging the Study of Culture and Religion: Pierre Bourdieu's Political Economy of Symbolic Power." *Sociology of Religion* 57, no. 1 (spring 1996): 71–85.

Sweet, Leonard I. *The Evangelical Tradition in America*. Macon, Ga: Mercer University Press, 1984.

Tannen, Deborah. *Talking from 9 to 5: How Women's and Men's Conversational Styles Affect Who Gets Heard, Who Gets Credit, and What Gets Done at Work*. New York: William Morrow, 1994.

Thumma, Scott. "Negotiating Religious Identity: The Case of the Gay Evangelical." *Sociological Analysis* 53 (winter): 333–347.

Wallace, Ruth A. *They Call Her Pastor: A New Role for Catholic Women*. Albany: SUNY Press, 1992.

Warner, R. Stephen. "Work in Progress toward a New Paradigm for the Sociological Study of Religion in the United States." *American Journal of Sociology* 98, no. 5 (March 1993): 1044–1093.

Wilcox, Clyde, and Elizabeth Adell Cook. "Evangelical Women and Feminism: Some Additional Evidence." *Women and Politics* 9, no. 2 (1989): 27–49.

Witt, Stacey L. "More Than a 'Slaving Wife': Evangelical College Women Encounter the New Woman of the 1920s." Unpublished essay presented at the Pew Fellow's Conference, April 8, 1995.

Wuthnow, Robert. *Meaning and Moral Order: Explorations in Cultural Analysis*. Berkeley: University of California Press, 1987.

———. *The Restructuring of American Religion*. Princeton: Princeton University Press, 1988.

———. *The Struggle for America's Soul: Evangelicals, Liberals, and Secularism*. Grand Rapids, Mich.: William B. Eerdmans, 1989.

———. *Rediscovering the Sacred: Perspectives on Religion in Contemporary Society*. Grand Rapids. Mich.: William B. Eerdmans, 1992.

———. *Producing the Sacred: An Essay on Public Religion*. Chicago: University of Illinois Press, 1994.

———. *Sharing the Journey*. New York: Free Press, 1994.

Wuthnow, Robert, and Marsha Witten. "New Directions in the Study of Culture." *American Review of Sociology*. Palo Alto, Calif.: Annual Reviews, 1988.

Index

About the Author

Julie Ingersoll is Assistant Professor of Religious Studies at the University of North Florida.